WORKBOOK

Awaken

YOUR SEXUALITY

A Guide to Connection and Intimacy after Addiction and Trauma

STEPHANIE S. COVINGTON, PhD, LCSW
VANESSA CARLISLE, PhD

Hazelden Publishing

Hazelden Publishing
Center City, Minnesota 55012
hazelden.org/bookstore

Printed in the United States of America

ISBN: 978-1-63634-093-7
Ebook ISBN: 978-1-63634-110-1

Editor's notes
Hazelden Publishing offers a variety of information on addiction and related areas. Our publications do not necessarily represent Hazelden Betty Ford Foundation's programs, nor do they officially speak for any Twelve Step organization.

The stories shared in this book were used with the consent of the individuals involved.

Readers should be aware that websites listed in this work may have changed or disappeared between when this work was written and when it is read.

29 28 27 26 25   1 2 3 4 5 6

Cover design: Sara Streifel, Think Creative Design
Typesetting and interior design: Sara Streifel, Think Creative Design
Developmental editor: Andy Lien
Production editor: Betty Christiansen

CONTENTS

A NOTE FROM ELIZABETH GILBERT

The book you hold in your hands is not only about addiction and sexual trauma (although those two subjects are covered in thorough, thoughtful, and deeply intelligent detail); it's also about pleasure. It's about our *right* to pleasure—no matter what we have done in the past or what has been done to us. It's about the honesty, safety, experimentation, and transparency that we deserve to experience both within our relationships and within our own private psyches. It's about how to set boundaries, how to understand what assault and abuse do to us on a physical and psychological level, how to *feel*, and how to be sexual while sober—perhaps for the first time in our lives, or at least in recent memory. It's about getting to define (and redefine) sensuality, intimacy, and commitment in any way that feels accurate to your own mind, body, and spirit.

What I appreciate most about this book is how careful the authors are to constantly bring the discussion back to *your* body, to *your* preferences, to *your* desires and needs and curiosities and hopes. When I work with newcomers in Twelve Step recovery, I often tell them that there are as many ways to get sober as there were to get high, and as many styles of recovery as there are people getting well. No one person has all the answers for another—and this book honors that truth with rare delicacy. We are reminded in these pages that there is no such thing as sexual "normalcy" and that we can change our minds and our behaviors as many times as we need to change in order to find our true selves. Furthermore, there is no gold standard that we must reach in order to become "good at sex," nor is there any bodily goal that we must achieve before we are allowed access to pleasure. No—we can awaken to the miracle of ourselves right here, right now, in this current form, in this current moment.

To learn how to feel our own feelings, to find our own opinions, to express our own desires, and to speak with our own voice—this is what recovery looks like. And this book shows you how to find that agency, that dignity, that literal ownership of yourself—within your ongoing recovery, and within the specific details of your own holy life.

INTRODUCTION

Now Is the Time

This workbook may be used on its own or as a companion to the book *Awaken Your Sexuality: A Guide to Connection and Intimacy after Addiction and Trauma*. Each chapter will assist you in identifying, cultivating, and enjoying the pleasures of your unique sexuality on the path to greater connection and intimacy. Regardless of relationship status, all of us can benefit from making time to awaken our senses, explore our values and desires, and take action to express our sexual selves with integrity.

You choose to awaken your sexuality because you are ready to experience the fullness of life. It happens when you decide you are ready to enjoy the creativity and pleasure of your unique body. That time can be now.

Our intended audience is anyone who identifies with the word *woman*. We recognize the majority of readers will have female anatomy and feel clear about their gender as women, also known as being cisgender. We welcome transgender women, nonbinary individuals who resonate with the experiences and challenges of women, and those who may not yet have labels or prefer no labels. Our use of *woman* is expansive, and we consider it a necessary shorthand, not an erasure of gender's complexity.

Gender and sexuality exist on their own spectrums, and variety is the most normal thing in the world. Heterosexual, bisexual, lesbian, pansexual, queer, questioning, and asexual women are all welcome in the exercises in this workbook. This workbook is for all kinds of women, nonbinary people, and gender-expansive people who have survived something difficult and want to feel better.

Throughout the exercises, you will meet a few women and nonbinary people who have lived through trauma, are recovering from harmful forms of substance use or compulsive behaviors, and are seeking a new, authentic connection to their sexuality. The stories included here come from women and nonbinary people we have known personally, worked with in therapy and coaching, and encountered over our combined years. We have changed details, timelines, and names to protect individual identities, and we have created composites from real women's experiences to help illuminate common concerns and pathways forward.

Why awaken your sexuality in the first place? If you have been frightened, confused, ashamed, or disconnected from your sexual self, feeling your own pleasure in a safe way may seem impossible. We assure you it is not. Our goal is to help you feel more pleasure and connection more often, in a way that supports and sustains you, with or without a partner.

Recovery is about living life fully and completely, and your sexual recovery is integral to the fullness of your life. While struggling with compulsive behaviors, problem use of a substance, or the symptoms of trauma (such as depression, anxiety, dissociation, and others), you likely have felt isolated and abandoned at times. In choosing to acknowledge and awaken your sexuality, you are embarking on an inner journey to reconnect with your best friend: your embodied self.

Each chapter of this workbook contains writing exercises to help you explore your unique sexual self, including your sexual past, present, and desired future. At the end of each chapter is a suggested somatic (body-based) activity for grounding and self-soothing. While each somatic activity can be practiced at any time, they are paired with specific content to support your emotional process. If you are completing this workbook in a group, you can practice these somatic activities together.

Some chapters may be more challenging than others, based on your personal history and current efforts at recovery. You can go at your own pace, on your own. Or you can create an accountability group and all complete the workbook on a schedule, such as one chapter per week. There is no wrong way to proceed. Please keep your workbook somewhere safe, so you can ensure your own privacy and freedom to complete the exercises honestly.

If you feel overwhelmed, experience symptoms of trauma, or find yourself wanting to return to using a substance you have stopped using, please slow down and consider asking for outside support from a loved one, support group, or a therapist. These exercises can be challenging, but they should not be traumatic to complete.

The same world that can cause us harm is also filled with wonder and mystery. Your unique sexuality is powerful and can bring you joy, pleasure, and deeper trust in yourself. It doesn't happen overnight, but it is absolutely worth the effort.

Checking In with My Sexuality Today

Let's begin by identifying how you feel about your sexual life as it is right now. After completing the *Awaken Your Sexuality Workbook*, you will be encouraged to return to this assessment to see how your feelings have changed.

Rate the following statements on a scale of 0 to 5, with 0 indicating no agreement and 5 indicating very strong agreement.

1. I am actively engaged in a form of recovery, such as therapy, a support/process group, Twelve Step group, harm reduction group, etc.

   0 1 2 3 4 5

2. I have experienced a substance use disorder, eating disorder, compulsive or addictive behaviors with spending, gambling, screen time, self-harm, work, relationships, sex, or something else that caused harm to myself and/or my loved ones.

   0 1 2 3 4 5

3. I believe that recovering sexually is important for my well-being.

   0 1 2 3 4 5

4. It seems like it has been a long time since I felt genuine sexual pleasure, or maybe I never have.

   0 1 2 3 4 5

5. As a child, I felt afraid to ask questions about sex or gender because it seemed like there could be negative consequences. As an adult, I feel avoidant or nervous talking about sexuality or gender.

   0 1 2 3 4 5

6. I have survived sexual trauma: sexual abuse, sexual assault, rape, or another form of sexual violence, such as workplace sexual harassment.

   0 1 2 3 4 5

7. I am not comfortable having sexual contact without alcohol or another substance.

   0 1 2 3 4 5

8. Sex with my partner(s) often doesn't feel good or gives me intrusive thoughts and/or memories.

   0 1 2 3 4 5

9. I haven't had a new sexual partner since I started recovering, and it makes me nervous to try again.

   0 1 2 3 4 5

10. I have experienced a relationship that diminished my self-worth and made me feel undesirable.

    0 1 2 3 4 5

11. My solo sex, or masturbation, is unsatisfying. Sometimes I avoid touching and exploring my own body.

    0 1 2 3 4 5

12. I have shame about how I have behaved sexually.

    0 1 2 3 4 5

If you answered almost all of the above with zeros, please feel free to put this workbook down and do something self-congratulatory! The rest of us still have plenty of work to do to honor our painful experiences, unravel negative beliefs about our sexual selves, and nourish our pleasure.

What we offer here is a gentle exploration of the ways sexuality can be a positive force in your life. In part 1, you will get reacquainted with your body, your feelings, and your memories, and you will consciously engage with your experience of desire and pleasure. In part 2, you will revisit your history and gain deeper understanding of how your sexual self has come to be and what changes you are making now. In part 3, you will practice articulating what you want, like, and dislike, and you will explore your current beliefs and values about sex, all with an eye toward your own pleasure. In part 4, you will develop the skills of connection and intimacy with yourself and others.

You do not have to eliminate your fear in order to be honest about your sexual feelings. Courage is acting honestly in spite of fear, knowing that the rewards of authentic self-knowledge will carry you forward on your journey of change. These rewards have a rhythm and momentum all their own—all your own.

So take courage. Please treat yourself with gentleness and patience and allow yourself to move at your own pace.

PART

1

Feelings: The Inner Journey

Each of us has an inner life and an outer life. Our inner life is who we are and how we feel inside; our outer life is how we interact with others. When we live in active addiction or are consumed by the pain of trauma, our inner and outer lives are out of balance. We don't always act on our feelings, and often we don't even know what our feelings are. We may be suffering so profoundly we cannot experience our full range of feeling. Part of recovery is getting our inner lives and our outer lives to reflect more of each other, and to experience a wider range of feelings.

In the next few chapters, we will be exploring some elements of early sexual recovery. You will be prompted to reflect on the effects of socialization in your life. You will endeavor to make some peace with your body, just as it is, at least for now. You will be learning about your genitals, and you will be guided to build a practice of self-pleasure. Through these exercises, you will become more aware of your sexual feelings, which exist separately from your partner or from anyone else. Your erotic life and sexual energy exist in their own right.

CHAPTER 1

The Past in the Present

Women totally, definitely, have been shamed and oppressed out of connecting with our real sexual selves.

Emily Nagoski, "My Lying Vagina, and the Lying Liars Who Lie About Her"

The subject of sexuality usually produces a paradoxical reaction: We are eager to know, but we are afraid of what we might find out. How did we come to such a confused state about something that is so basic to human existence?

Our present sexual feelings and actions do not exist in a vacuum. They are molded and influenced by everything that has happened to us in the past. By working with our past and honestly naming all that has happened to us—our gender socialization within our family, our childhood experiences, our adolescent sexual experiences, our choice of partners, our sexual behavior prior to the decision to recover—we can move into a new level of sexual freedom and expansion. When this happens, our sexual feelings and actions will arise from the present moment, not from the mixed messages, pain, confusion, or dissociation we had in the past.

My Sexual Self-Image

1. Think back to your childhood. How did you learn about what it meant to be a woman or man? Did your family or caregivers talk with you about nonbinary, transgender, or any other gender-expansive expression? Do you remember any specific instance in which you were told how to behave according to your gender?

Example:

When I was six and my brother was a baby, my mom told me, "Boys have a penis and girls have a vagina." We never talked about gender; I don't think I even heard the word until I was a teenager. But there were a lot of jokes in the house about Mom's way of doing things versus Dad's way. Dad's way was always more fun and less safe. I definitely got in trouble for ripping my clothes playing touch football at school and was told that I was unladylike.

2. Would you describe your parents or caregivers as open and communicative about sexuality? Would you describe them as closed off or not approachable about sexual topics? Perhaps a mix of both? Do you remember feeling mostly comfortable or uncomfortable talking to your parents or caregivers about sex?

3. When do you remember becoming curious about your own body or about sexuality in general? Did you feel that your curiosity was similar to your peers'? Why or why not?

4. Do you remember feeling pressure to be "good at sex" as a young person? Can you identify where that pressure was coming from?

Authentic Sex Talk

One way to honestly examine your beliefs and assumptions about what you need and what you want sexually is dialogue with another person or a safe group. Many people have not experienced safe conversations about sex and sexuality with knowledgeable sources.

5. Where did you get your information about sex as a younger person? (Check all that apply.)

    - ☐ I had safe adults in my life who would answer my questions.
    - ☐ I received comprehensive sexual education in school.
    - ☐ I received abstinence-only education in school.
    - ☐ I had friends who taught me about sex.
    - ☐ I had a boyfriend/girlfriend/partner who taught me about sex.
    - ☐ I had traumatic or abusive experiences that taught me about sex.
    - ☐ I learned about sex from Hollywood movies, pornography, TV shows, or other media.
    - ☐ I read books or articles to teach myself about sex.
    - ☐ I learned about sex through ______________________________.

Michelle

Michelle, thirty-nine, is a stay-at-home mom to two small children and lives in a mostly white suburb of a major city. Michelle and her husband, Chris, got married after dating for a few years, and they have a busy social life and a beautiful home. During the COVID-19 pandemic lockdowns, Michelle stopped working to care for their children full time. She also slid from several drinks a week to heavy drinking nearly every night, combined with prescription medication for insomnia and anxiety.

When Michelle was a child, Michelle's mother managed to keep a household together while Michelle's father drank before, during, and after work. Because he wasn't physically violent, and their material needs and wants were met, Michelle has always considered herself lucky, and her childhood in an alcoholic family "not that bad."

Now that Michelle is in recovery for her own alcohol use disorder and symptoms from a past traumatic sexual assault, she is taking a closer look at her childhood. She remembers having one conversation with her mother, when she got her period, where her mother admonished her to "lock your knees together." Michelle struggles to remember how she ever learned about her own body or sex itself. She believes herself to be more sexually educated than her mother, but since they never spoke about it, she's not really sure.

6. When you reflect on how you learned about sexuality, gender, and sex, what feelings come up for you?

If you never received comprehensive sexual education, you may want to pursue it now, as an adult. It is never too late to learn more about sex, gender, and sexuality, because new research is happening all the time. We recommend the resources at Planned Parenthood's "Sex Ed To-Go for Students" for a free option to get you started. While the classes are listed by grade level, many of the topics can be helpful for people of any age.

Tamara

Tamara, sixty-three, is a tenured professor of history and African American studies at a large university, where she has won numerous teaching awards. She often speaks publicly about her experiences of tokenism and misogynoir (the combined force of anti-Black racism and misogyny directed toward Black women) at conferences for women in academia. Her books are used in college courses across the country.

Years ago, Tamara had a serious car accident and was prescribed an opioid pain medication while she recovered from a series of back surgeries. Tamara had accepted that she would likely be dependent on pain pills for the rest of her life, but something changed when she went through her divorce with her wife, Alisha. She began buying pills to add to her regular prescription, and she became addicted.

Tamara grew up without words to identify her feelings and experiences, and she always felt like an outsider in her homophobic Christian family. Still, she maintains a deep love for her mother, Anne, who is now living with her and experiencing a new level of physical dependence.

Anne is a devout Christian who has never been comfortable with Tamara's sexual orientation, even though she was always kind and respectful to Alisha, Tamara's ex-wife. Tamara and her mother live amicably, but Tamara can feel the difference.

"I love Mom, but I am smaller in spirit around her," Tamara tells her therapist.

7. What did your early social environment teach you to feel about yourself?

Example:
I learned to keep a lot of myself a secret. I was "too much" if I wasn't careful. I shouldn't speak my mind.

Your body?

Your gender?

Your sexual orientation?

Your sexual feelings?

Discovering Our Sexual Selves

We all received messages about our worth as human beings and how our gender and sexuality affected our worth. The message implicit in all the exercises you will encounter in this workbook is that sexuality is much more than sexual behavior. Sexuality can be a lifelong process of discovery, an important part of who we are and how we are in the world regardless of how much desire we do or don't feel and whether or not we have a partner.

8. Complete the following statements:

   As a result of engaging with the exercises in this workbook, I hope to feel:

   I hope to experience:

I hope to learn:

I hope to change:

Somatic Practice: Opening to Possibility

The word *soma* means "body." Somatic practices are body-based activities that may involve movement, breathing, or self-touch. They can assist you in feeling more grounded, calm, and present. There are many ways to connect with your body, and the practices suggested here are a few that we have found useful to address the feelings that can arise when thinking deeply about our history, behavior, and sexuality. Please feel invited to do any self-soothing activity that works for you.

For this brief practice, sit on a chair with both feet on the floor and your hands resting comfortably in your lap. Your eyes can be open or closed. Turn your head all the way to the right. As you inhale slowly and deeply, imagine drawing a rainbow in an arc overhead, from your right shoulder to your left, with the tip of your nose. While inhaling, begin to move your head to draw the arc. When you get to the top of the arc, begin to exhale, so that when you arrive at your left side, you are empty of breath.

This time, inhale as you draw the rainbow from the left all the way over to the right. At the top of the arc, begin to exhale so you arrive at your right shoulder at the end of your exhale. The slower you are able to breathe, and the smoother you can make your movement, the more relaxing the practice will be. Do not worry about getting it "right" or creating the perfect rainbow shape—the practice of coordinating your breath and your movement is enough.

CHAPTER 2

Inauthenticity and Contradictions

We have had the truth of our bodies withheld from us or distorted; we have been kept in ignorance of our most intimate places. Our instincts have been punished . . . it has been difficult, too, to know the lies of our complicity from the lies we believed.

Adrienne Rich, *On Lies, Secrets, and Silence: Selected Prose 1966–1975*

Sometimes we get so lost in being sexual the way our partner wants us to, or the way we were taught we should, or the way we've seen in movies or shows, or the only way we know how, that we aren't able to sense what brings us our own true pleasure. When we perform sexually for others more than we authentically engage with our body's likes and dislikes, we can get lost and out of balance.

This is not to say that being generous with our partners is a problem—on the contrary. *Referred pleasure*, or the joy we feel when our partner is experiencing their own pleasure, is a real thing. Attentiveness, generosity, and joy at being a "giver" are lovely expressions of sexuality when they are freely offered and felt.

What we seek is self-awareness, so we can be fully at choice whenever we are sexual. In this chapter, we will explore the ways we have been taught to live in denial of our sexuality and begin to reconnect honestly with our own sources of pleasure.

Silencing the Inner Voice

Being honest, especially with ourselves, is a necessary first step toward changing our patterns.

In families where shame drives a large amount of everyone's behavior, such as families with addiction, abuse, or other painful issues, it is common to see something called a "no-talk rule." A no-talk rule applies to anything that would disrupt the status quo: Children do not talk about a parent's addiction, parents do not talk about a partner's infidelity or abuse, and so on.

The no-talk rule is also a familiar fixture in most of our sexual lives. This rule has a variety of forms: If you need to talk about sex, it's not okay; it's no good if you have to ask for what you want. If your partner really loved you, you would get just what you wanted and needed in bed. When the right person comes along, it's going to be perfect. If it's not perfect, there must be something wrong with you, your body, or your technique. If it was easy at first, but something has changed, there is something wrong with you—better avoid bringing it up. And on and on.

Let's take a few minutes to identify and explore the forms of the no-talk rule that we remember from childhood, and those that may be at work in our lives today.

1. Fill in the chart below one column at a time. First, identify a no-talk rule you remember from childhood. It may be about anything, not just sexual subjects. If you lived in more than one household, you can list the rules separately, as they may have been different. Then, decide whether you are still abiding by these rules in any form in your life today. Last, you can list the way a no-talk rule may be part of your life as an adult.

No-talk rule from childhood	Do I still follow this? How so?	New no-talk rule
EXAMPLES:		
Don't say anything about Mom's drinking to anyone.	*No. I talk about it all the time in recovery group.*	*Don't talk about my own drinking or recovery with people who are still drinking.*
Don't ask about sex.	*Yes. I don't talk to anyone about my real questions or concerns, not even my doctor.*	*Same. Don't ask about sex.*
Don't talk about having a crush on another girl.	*Somewhat. Still not "out" to everyone in my life.*	*Don't be an "in your face" lesbian.*

continued on next page

No-talk rule from childhood	Do I still follow this? How so?	New no-talk rule

How do you feel when you reflect on your entries to this list?

Sex as a Means to an End

The things we do when we are in the grip of addiction and trauma can be extremely harmful to ourselves and other people. We usually believe that the ends justify the means. Part of any recovery process is taking responsibility and accountability for the harms we have caused to others.

At the same time, physical and sexual abuse are unfortunately not uncommon experiences. These experiences affect nearly every part of us: our sense of self, our cognition, our physical health, our faith in our own perceptions, our relationships, and so on.

Sexual recovery can mean facing experiences where we were not given a choice—where we were physically unsafe, overpowered, or betrayed by someone who was supposed to care for us. Sexual recovery can mean facing a very painful history of sexual experiences we wish had not happened.

Also, sexual recovery can mean facing sexual choices we would not repeat, or ways we pressured others and used them as a means to an end, much like we had been used.

Ash

Ash, thirty-three, a nonbinary person who was assigned female at birth, was sexually abused by their stepfather from age four until ten, when they told a teacher at school what was happening. Ash was removed from their home. Ash's mother was addicted to heroin and was not able to create a safe home for Ash to return to.

Ash bounced from one foster care home to another, eventually spending two years in a girls' group home until they turned eighteen. At the home, Ash had a sexual relationship with a male staff member, who gave them more freedoms than the other girls. "I wasn't popular," Ash remembers. "But I never felt like I fit in with the girls anyway, so I didn't care."

As a child enduring sexual abuse, Ash learned that if they lay still and quiet, the terrible moment would end quicker, and afterward their stepfather would treat them very nicely for a day or two. Unconsciously, this lesson stuck. As a teenager, Ash tried to take control of their situation by creating relationships with people who had power over their life: sleeping with a staff member at their group home to gain more freedoms and having sex with a manager at their job to smooth over problems they'd created while they were high.

Ash had sex in exchange for drugs, a place to sleep, a meal, anything that would help them survive to the next day and the next opportunity to get high. Ash learned early that sex could get them something they wanted or needed. Sex they didn't want seemed like a small price to pay for survival.

2. Have you ever had sex or let someone believe you wanted to have sex, for the purpose of getting something you needed or wanted? That something could have been tangible, like a place to sleep. It could also be something less tangible, like "for my partner to stop asking me for sex" or "for someone to notice me."

   List these experiences below and then rate how you feel about them on a scale of 0 (very uncomfortable) to 5 (very comfortable), adding a description of how you feel. Reflect on what makes you comfortable or uncomfortable about these experiences.

Experience	**Rating 0–5**	**Reflection**
EXAMPLE: *Sex with my boyfriend's friend to make him jealous after he cheated on me.*	*2—somewhat uncomfortable*	*I wouldn't do it again, but it did make me feel better in the moment.*

Have you felt used by another person sexually? This can include abuse, but it can also include friendships that seemed to have an ulterior motive, professional connections that felt exploitative, and so on. As you describe your experience below, please remember to be gentle with yourself and only write down what you feel safe to share today.

Our accountability processes need to reflect the truth of our own behavior, and, at the same time, we need to be clear about the behavior of others that was *their* responsibility. If your own history still feels somewhat unclear, that is understandable. In the coming chapters, you will receive continuing support for sorting out your own responsibility from that of others.

Social Lies

Social lies are the lies that our family, community, culture, and larger society teach us. All of us are affected by these myths, whether we believe them personally or not. Social lies become institutionalized—they are passed down from parent to child; taught in schools, religions, and legal systems; and reinforced by governmental policy and law. It is important that we become aware of the detrimental effects these lies have on our lives.

3. Following are five sets of opposing beliefs. Take a minute to imagine yourself having the first belief. Write down how you *feel* and what you would *do* if you believed in your gut that Belief A were true. Then do the same for Belief B.

SET 1

Belief A: Addiction makes you a bad person.

- How would you feel if you were convinced of Belief A?

- How would you live *this week* if you thought Belief A were true?

Belief B: Addiction can lead to behavior that is not in alignment with a person's values. However, with time and effort, a person can make amends and change their behavior to reflect their integrity.

- How would you feel if you were confident of Belief B?

- How would you live *this week* if you thought Belief B were true?

SET 2

Belief A: Some bodies are better than others.

- How would you feel if you were convinced of Belief A?

- How would you live *this week* if you thought Belief A were true?

Belief B: Everyone's body is equally deserving of life, love, and care.

- How would you feel if you were confident of Belief B?

- How would you live *this week* if you thought Belief B were true?

SET 3

Belief A: Pleasure is not that important.

- How would you feel if you were convinced of Belief A?

- How would you live *this week* if you thought Belief A were true?

Belief B: Pleasure is important because it is an honest expression of ourselves.

- How would you feel if you were confident of Belief B?

- How would you live *this week* if you thought Belief B were true?

SET 4

Belief A: Gender is irrelevant.

- How would you feel if you were convinced of Belief A?

- How would you live *this week* if you thought Belief A were true?

Belief B: As we work to end gender-based oppression and violence, we can honor that expressions of gender are an important part of our social world.

- How would you feel if you were confident of Belief B?

- How would you live *this week* if you thought Belief B were true?

SET 5

Belief A: There is an ideal way to be sexual, and you are failing at it.

- How would you feel if you were convinced of Belief A?

- How would you live *this week* if you thought Belief A were true?

Belief B: The ideal way to be sexual is defined by each person for themselves, according to their values, desires, capacities, and, if applicable, communication with consenting partners.

- How would you feel if you were confident of Belief B?

- How would you live *this week* if you thought Belief B were true?

The Hope of Truth

The first step in a sexual recovery process is to be honest about your sexual feelings, whether they are clear or cloudy, familiar or new. Being honest takes courage and the willingness to find out what it is that you want and feel, and to discover a way to express it.

Becoming who you want to be sexually is about becoming whole; it is about becoming a person with choice, empowered to risk and change. It is about integrating your feelings and actions into a seamless web of self, bridging the gap between your inner feelings and your outer actions. It is about remembering that feeling good in our bodies is a wonderful way to be alive.

4. Try to remember a time when you felt sexual pleasure, bliss, or delight, either alone or with a partner. Write out the story here, adding in as many details as you can remember.

   If you don't feel you've had this experience, write a scenario you'd like to experience in the future.

Somatic Practice: Palms Up, Palms Down

Sit comfortably with your back straight. Close your eyes or lower your eyelids and focus on your breathing. Take a slow, deep breath while counting to four. Then exhale slowly, counting to four.

Do this four more times until your breathing is slow and relaxed.

Keep breathing slowly and evenly. Hold your hands gently in front of you with your palms up, and imagine them holding all the negative or upsetting thoughts and feelings you have had today.

Now turn your palms down. Imagine yourself emptying your hands of all the negative or upsetting things you've been carrying today. Let go of them.

Keep breathing slowly. Now turn your palms up. Your palms are up and open to receive positive energy, positive thoughts, and positive feelings. Your palms are open to receive support and help.

Slowly open your eyes and relax your hands.

Anytime you need to let go of something negative and receive the positive, you can take a few minutes to do this activity.

CHAPTER 3

The Flow of Desire and Pleasure

Desire is not simply a desire of each self for its self-pleasure. But what is it for?

Possibly, if it is for anything, desire is for the experience of the journey toward and joining in something that thereby becomes greater than the separate selves. Desire in the larger sense affirms our connection and being "a part of" rather than "apart from." It leads to expansion rather than satisfaction; the former suggests growth, life, and openness; the latter suggests stasis.

Judith V. Jordan, "Clarity in Connection: Empathic Knowing, Desire, and Sexuality"

Knowing when you feel desire and being relatively comfortable expressing it are vital steps on your journey toward sexual empowerment, but that's only the beginning.

Importantly, an overemphasis on feeling sexual desire can backfire. This is because sexual desire waxes and wanes based on many factors, some under our control, many not. Your sexuality may involve a lot of *spontaneous desire*: You may see a sexy person in the grocery store and instantly fantasize about their naked body. Or you may require more context, more attention, and more pleasure before your desire emerges—this is called *responsive desire*. Most people tend toward one type or the other, spontaneous or responsive, and it is normal to experience them both. It is also normal to feel neither! It doesn't mean you are unable to feel pleasure.

The only form of desire our culture seems to care about is spontaneous desire, and it is presumed to be part of a "normal" sexual life. The truth is, no matter how much or how little spontaneous desire you feel for a partner, your unique sexuality can respond to pleasure.

This chapter will help you understand your patterns from the past, identify challenges you may face in experiencing desire and pleasure, and empower you to seek the pleasure that works for you.

What Is Desire?

There is no wrong way to feel desire—you may feel it at inopportune times, for inappropriate people, quietly or loudly, quickly or slowly, like a lightning strike or a slow creep of lava. Your desire can take many shapes. The idea that there is one right way to experience desire (spontaneously, at the sight of a partner!) is not only unhelpful; it creates a lot of shame and stress. Sexual desire is a set of feelings and sensations, an internal experience.

1. Write three to five sentences for each of the following thoughts:

   I know I'm feeling desire when . . .

   Desire makes me . . .

   If I fully believed there was nothing wrong with how I experience desire, then . . .

My fantasy life consists of . . .

I believe that the relationship between desire and pleasure is . . .

Nova

Nova, twenty-five, works at a strip club and runs a peer-support recovery group for sex workers. She grew up in an intentional spiritual community and was raised in a nontraditional household of nearly twenty people. She was taught about her body, sex, and procreation without shame, and she was comfortable in sexual exploration as a teenager with both boys and girls.

During her early years working at the club, Nova felt a large pressure to "party" with her customers, and she developed some destructive habits to cope. Many nights, she would drink at pace with the men she was entertaining, black out, and either wake up at home without knowing how she got there or, worse, with someone she hadn't consciously consented to have sex with. To stop the blackouts, Nova followed the advice of another dancer at her club and added uppers to the mix, including cocaine and methamphetamine.

Nova learned to use her sexual attractiveness to make a living. When she had sex with men outside the club during her active addiction, it wasn't important whether she actually desired the man or the sexual experience. She became an expert at pleasing men; she was alert and responsive to their sexual needs and desires, but she did not know what pleased her or whether she was feeling sexual desire. Her body's signals were often unclear, especially when she was using alcohol, cocaine, and methamphetamine, but she still wasn't sure how much desire she was feeling even after she got sober.

"I got used to drinking and being high to make sex happen," Nova says. "I know how to act sexy; I do it for a living! But deep down I don't feel that sexy within myself. It's a performance for customers. I'm not sure who I am sexually, or what I want, or if I even have real sexual feelings of my own."

Nova has been sober for more than a year. On the advice of another person in recovery, Nova began to methodically attempt to find new pleasures for every one of her five senses. She bought a new, soft blanket that she loves to touch. She lights candles in her room instead of turning on the overhead light to delight her vision.

More than a year ago, Nova was able to push through the difficulty of detox and maintain sobriety with her tenacity and self-awareness. This new phase will require additional skills: gentleness, self-compassion, and curiosity. Nova's desire to experience pleasure through her senses has guided her to another level of recovery.

You do not need to experience spontaneous sexual desire to be able to experience pleasure. Your desire can take the form of seeking new ways to connect with your own body and feel the sensations that delight you. The more you notice what pleases you, the more you can cultivate those pleasures. Rather than relying on spontaneous sexual desire, let your desire for connection and knowledge of self be your guide.

2. Every day for the next five days, do your best to notice the information your senses bring to you. If you have a disability that impacts any of the senses listed here, please adjust the exercise so it is right for you. Answer the questions below to help identify what you notice, and feel free to jot down more notes of your own.

   Day One: Focus on your sight.

   Date: ____________________

   What do you see? Notice if it pleases you, seems beautiful, or piques your curiosity.

Day Two: Focus on your hearing.

Date: ____________

What sounds do you notice in your daily life? Which ones are pleasing, and which ones are grating to you? Can you cultivate more pleasant sounds, like playing music or listening to birds in the morning?

Day Three: Focus on your senses of smell and taste.

Date: ____________

Smell and taste are deeply linked, and noticing this link is part of the practice. What scents and smells do you notice? Are they pleasant for you? Do any of them make your mouth water? How does your food smell, and how does it taste? Take some time to notice.

Day Four: Focus on your sense of touch.

Date: ____________________

Notice the textures you are in contact with. Where do you feel softness, ridges, sharp edges, hard surfaces? Which textures are you most interested in?

Day Five: Focus on *interoception*, or sensing inside your body.

Date: ____________________

Throughout the day, check in with your body on the inside. How is your throat, stomach, lower gut? Where do you feel muscle tension, and where do you feel relaxation?

Tuning in to the inside of your body is a great way to reconnect with your inner sensations, which can open doors to your erotic experience. Some even find these exercises spark more spontaneous sexual desire!

Understanding Sexual Arousal

The *dual control model* describes sexual arousal as a system that has both an accelerator and a brake, like a car. They are separate functions, the brake and the accelerator, and every person is going to have different levels of sensitivity in each. A person with a sensitive accelerator may feel turned on easily, but if they also have a sensitive brake, they can be turned off just as quickly. Sometimes, both seem to happen simultaneously.

According to Dr. Emily Nagoski, author and sex researcher, it is most common for women to be somewhere in the middle level of sensitivity in both their accelerator and their brake.[1] However, it shouldn't be surprising that addiction, compulsive behaviors, and traumatic experiences can powerfully affect anyone's accelerating and braking systems. (So can many mood-stabilizing medications, giving birth, menopause, gender transition, and so much more.)

3. See if you can list one or more answers to the following questions.

   What hits your accelerator at this time in your life? What turns you on?

   Example:

   Accelerator: Being told I'm beautiful, especially when I don't have makeup on.

   What hits your brake? What turns you off?

   Example:

   Brake: When my partner is on their phone instead of spending time with me.

Is there anything that takes pressure off your brake so you can feel your accelerator more easily?

Example:

Take pressure off brake: When my partner cleans our room before date night.

Is there something that activates both at the same time?

Example:

Both: When we argue. I want to be close and I don't want to be close at the same time.

Arousal nonconcordance happens when our body's response to something does not match our feelings, and it is *totally normal*. Arousal nonconcordance is an especially important concept for survivors of sexual trauma. Many women and gender-diverse people feel shame about how their body responded while they were being assaulted. A genital response during an assault does not mean the survivor enjoyed the experience. Physical arousal *can be* deeply connected to pleasure and desire, but it can also be elusive—happening without pleasure, or not happening when we are sure we are feeling desire.

4. Take a few minutes to identify your own body's physiological arousal responses. What normally happens to your body when you are aroused? Some examples might be vaginal lubrication, erection of the clitoris, heart beating faster, or feeling warm.

Has there ever been a time when you felt that your emotions and your physical response were not matching well? Maybe you wanted to be sexual, but your body was not getting aroused. Or maybe your body responded with sexual arousal to a situation that you weren't emotionally comfortable with. This is your experience of arousal nonconcordance. Write your memory here:

Physical and Emotional Challenges

Virtually all people are capable of feeling pleasure. Sexual pleasure may be more difficult for people in recovery for a host of reasons. Some include the physical challenges of recovery, such as returning to health after withdrawal, and some may be seen as more emotional challenges, such as processing loss and grief.

Physical and emotional challenges are deeply interconnected. Emotions are a physical experience, and physical experiences affect our emotions.

5. To identify some of the challenges you are navigating that may be affecting your sexual life, check all that apply below. If a statement only partially applies, check the box and rephrase the statement in a way that is more true for you. If you don't see a particular challenge stated here, feel free to add it to the list.

    - ☐ I have some physical health concerns related to my recovery.
    - ☐ I regularly feel very fatigued.
    - ☐ I struggle to eat adequate meals during the day.
    - ☐ I am taking medications for depression, anxiety, or another mental health concern that may be affecting my sexual responses. Or I am experiencing symptoms of depression, anxiety, or another mental health concern that interferes with my sexual responses.
    - ☐ I do not have reliable, safe gynecological care.
    - ☐ I experience pain or dissociation when trying to be sexual with someone.
    - ☐ I am not sure how to confidently engage with someone sexually without the use of alcohol or other substances.
    - ☐ I do not sleep well.
    - ☐ I have a history of sexual abuse or trauma that interferes with my sexual feelings in the present.
    - ☐ I struggle to accept my body the way it is.
    - ☐ I feel afraid or avoidant when talking to a partner about sex.
    - ☐ I don't have access to a private space where I feel safe to express my sexuality.
    - ☐ I have experienced a significant loss (the death of a loved one, job loss, loss of custody of children, and so on) and have strong feelings, such as grief, anger, despair, or loneliness.
    - ☐ I struggle with: ____

      ____.

Whether you checked one or many boxes above, remember that the challenges we face affect our sexual feelings. We are not broken or damaged. We need to approach ourselves with tenderness and curiosity as we recover.

Seeking Pleasure

Remember that sexual recovery is not a linear process. It can help to think of it more like an upward spiral. You will likely return to many of the same issues, memories, and questions you had at the beginning of your recovery, but in more nuanced ways, with more skills to navigate them, and with a greater sense of who you are and where you are headed. As you put in the work and move up the spiral over time, more pleasure and connection become available to you.

FIGURE 1

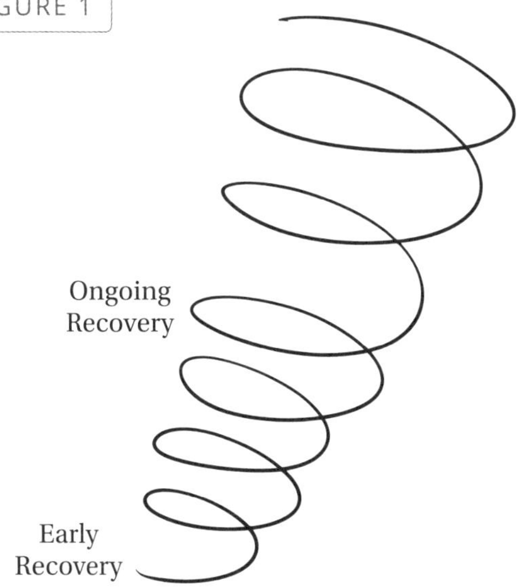

6. We have identified a few challenges that are part of sexual recovery. Now we can identify some of your strengths and celebrate ways that you are changing. These are the gifts of the upward spiral. Use the space below to describe the progress you have experienced in awakening your sexuality so far.

   Example:

   I realized my husband and I were trying to squeeze sex into the last few minutes of being awake after very long days, and that was hitting the brake for me. I needed a conversation about taking our time and prioritizing pleasure together. I was nervous to ask to talk about it, but I did it!

The Courage to Relearn

It's never too late to connect with yourself. Allow yourself to feel your feelings and to be exactly where you are in the process. Comfort yourself with the fact that no matter your past, you can do what you need to do to feel safe as you explore your sexual self, here today. Recovering sexually takes courage, as you may need to relearn a lot about yourself, your beliefs, your desires, and what actually brings you pleasure.

7. Make a list of things that can help you feel safe and relaxed overall.

   Examples:

   Being able to shut my door and trust no one will barge in

   Knowing I have enough money to cover an emergency bill

   A hug from my friend

   Doing a puzzle

   Now make a list of things that can help you feel sexy, desirous, or attuned to pleasure:

   Examples:

   Dancing to music

   Wearing my leather boots

   Reading a romance novel

   A great meal

Take a few minutes to write down the thoughts that come up when you look at these lists side by side. Do the lists share anything in common? Are they at odds in any way? What feelings arise when you look at what you wrote down?

Somatic Practice: Patting the Body

This practice can be used anytime you need to feel more grounded or present in your body. You can stand or do the practice seated. Begin by imagining the way someone who cares for you might pat you on the arm if they were saying "atta girl!" (or any other kind words of affirmation). Now recreate that patting motion with your own hands, starting on your shoulders and upper arms. Keep your fingers together and relax your wrists. The intended effect of this motion is a feeling of aliveness and reassurance.

Pat gently but firmly, moving slowly down your body, paying attention to every part of your body that you can reach comfortably. If your mind wanders or begins to judge you, your body, or the practice, try to return your attention to the sensation of the activity, and speak kind words to yourself.

When you have given your body as many pats as you'd like, sit quietly for a minute or two and notice the sensations and feelings that are present now.

CHAPTER 4

Accepting Your Body

A PRAYER OF GRATITUDE AND COMMITMENT

Dear body, thank you for being in witness to my life. For your unwavering accompaniment. For the blessing you have offered by keeping me alive, keeping me here on earth, so that I may do the work we came to do. I have faith in our partnership, in our ability to be in right relationship both with each other and with the world around us. I commit to acknowledging and honoring your wisdom, to knowing you better each day. I acknowledge your hurt and pain, so that you no longer need to numb, and I invite our community to hold us, so that we may grieve together.

You are my best friend and I am yours.

You are my best friend and I am yours.

You are my best friend. And I am yours.

Meenadchi, *Decolonizing Nonviolent Communication,* 2nd ed.

It is not an overstatement to say it has been normalized for everyone to dislike some part of their body. Negative feelings about our bodies reflect our culture's emphasis on the importance of appearance, especially for women who seek to embody a feminine ideal. Despite many years of feminist activity addressing "beauty culture," privilege still accrues to white, slim, smooth, hair-free, unwrinkled, airbrushed young women, with curves permitted only in a few key places. (At the same time, these very women often report negative feelings about their bodies!)

Comparing ourselves to a body that seems more valuable sets us up to feel inadequate and less lovable. Likewise, feeling better about our bodies because we are achieving "perfection" (measured against others' imperfect bodies) is not the same thing as true self-acceptance.

In this chapter, we will address the messages we have received about our bodies and replace old ideas with self-acceptance. Self-acceptance at any level depends in part on knowing and accepting our body as it is, even if we intend to make changes.

Admiring our body and reveling in what it can do rather than focusing on its shortcomings or perceived flaws comes on the heels of this acceptance; it may happen more quickly for some of us than for others, depending on our unique combination of experiences and identities.

Making Peace with Your Body

Arati

Arati, twenty-nine, is a graduate student studying statistics and a single mom of a three-year-old son. Her parents immigrated to the United States from India just before Arati was born, and she considers herself close to her family, even though they were initially unsupportive of her having a child without a husband.

Arati has relied on her parents for financial support and childcare, but she keeps them in the dark about her queer identity and whom she dates.

Arati does not have a formal diagnosis of attention-deficit/hyperactivity disorder (ADHD) that would indicate a need for treatment. She began taking Adderall to sustain focus on her schoolwork for long periods of time. Arati has now become reliant on higher and higher doses of Adderall for energy and concentration. She buys it from a classmate, which is easy and common among her peers on campus. At night, Arati drinks wine to relax—sometimes a bottle, usually more.

Recently, Arati met an attractive person at a meetup for LGBTQ+ students in STEM. The new person flirted easily, seemed excited to get to know Arati, and asked her out on a date.

As Arati started getting ready for her date and getting her son ready to go to his grandparents' house, she caught herself in the mirror. She panicked. She realized that even with her years of sexual experience, she felt awkward, unsexy, and disconnected from her own body.

Arati tried to fix her posture, suck in her belly, and roll her shoulders back. It made no difference. She spent a long time picking out clothes that hid most of her body, feeling critical and despairing the whole time.

Arati took extra Adderall, which made her feel slightly nauseated, so she skipped most of dinner. Then, she drank more alcohol than usual, to calm her anxieties.

Arati enjoyed the new person but felt out of control. When she said goodnight to her date, she pushed their hands away from her waist, ashamed of the softness of her body.

How we regard our body affects our sexual experiences. Negative beliefs about our body can affect our ability to relax into pleasurable experiences. Knowing what you really think about your body is the first step.

1. Rate the following statements from 0 (strongly disagree) to 5 (strongly agree).

   I have a positive regard for my body.

   0 1 2 3 4 5

   I have memories of negative statements about my body from my parents, caregivers, or other adults I had regular contact with.

   0 1 2 3 4 5

   I heard negative statements about my body from siblings, friends, or other people my age.

   0 1 2 3 4 5

   When I look in the mirror, I am pleased at what I see.

   0 1 2 3 4 5

My body has "problem areas."

0 1 2 3 4 5

I enjoy touching my own body.

0 1 2 3 4 5

I have trouble recognizing my body's needs: I may forget to eat, use the bathroom, etc., until I feel extreme urgency.

0 1 2 3 4 5

I choose to push through exhaustion rather than take my rest.

0 1 2 3 4 5

I want more control over my body.

0 1 2 3 4 5

I make time in my day to care for my body.

0 1 2 3 4 5

My body betrays me.

0 1 2 3 4 5

I have experienced discrimination based on characteristics of my body—skin color, body size, disability, etc.

0 1 2 3 4 5

I sometimes wish I didn't have to deal with having a body at all.

0 1 2 3 4 5

Take a few minutes to reflect on your answers to the above. How would you describe your relationship with your own body overall?

Listening to Your Body's Messages

The key to a more neutral, even positive regard for your body is conscious effort toward becoming more aware of how your body feels, what it needs, and what it can do rather than how it looks or what it can't do. When you listen to your body's messages, you begin to work with rather than against yourself.

We won't pretend that your relationship to your body exists in a vacuum—in fact, most of the negative things you say to yourself are the result of violently cruel biases that you did not invent. The systems that enact body-based oppression won't be changed overnight.

However, we believe that we increase our collective capacity to change those systems by cultivating at least a neutral relationship with our own bodies and positive regard for the bodies of others.

Here are a few practical techniques for making better friends with your body. It is safe to cultivate daily awareness of your relationship with your body, feel your body's sensations, and see what your body looks like. If you are used to a lot of negative internal chatter when looking in the mirror, the following exercise is for you.

2. Find a time when you are alone and undisturbed.

   Take everything off and stand naked in front of a full-length mirror. If you don't have a full-length mirror, you can do this exercise with a hand mirror, moving it slowly around your body so you can see each part, one at a time. You don't need to prepare your body for this activity—you get to have hair, odor, pimples, dry skin. Let your body exist however it does, right in this moment.

The point of this exercise is just to look, not to evaluate. Avoid weighing yourself before or after this exercise; avoid trying to make your body look "better" in the mirror. See if you can look at your body with new eyes—eyes that appreciate your aliveness.

If this causes you significant distress, please back off and get some support. This exercise can be challenging, but it shouldn't send you into panic. If looking at your body makes you feel panicked or disgusted, it's time to seek some more support.

Right now, all you are doing is looking at your own body with soft curiosity. Imagine you appreciate everything your body has done to keep you alive to this moment. What do you see?

3. After you have spent some time getting to know your body in the mirror with gentleness, you can take more action toward acceptance.

   Reread "A Prayer of Gratitude and Commitment" from page 45.

   Using your hands, move slowly over your body, thanking each part. First do it verbally. No matter how awkward you might feel, see if you can take a full tour, saying something kind and expressing some gratitude toward every part of you.

   Sit quietly for a minute and see how you feel. Listen to your body.

Now write down five expressions of gratitude to your body.

Examples:

Thank you, feet, for helping me to walk and run and dance.

Thank you, neck, for supporting my head.

Thank you, shoulders, for carrying my bags around.

You can add to this list anytime, and you can read it whenever you need to.

Now we will extend the gentle, curious gaze of the first mirror exercise specifically to your genitals. Different versions of the following exercise have become popular touchstones for those who are interested in sexuality.

You may be tempted to skip this exercise, especially if you have done it a time or two in the past, but we encourage you to make the effort here and now. Doing this exercise as part of your sexual recovery is about becoming the person who knows your body best.

4. Do this exercise when you are alone and feel safe and undisturbed. You can approach it with two objectives: to see what's there and to feel what happens when you touch various parts of yourself.

   For this exercise, you will need a hand mirror and a flashlight.

   - Sit propped up, maybe with pillows behind your back, and your knees bent and open. You may want to also put pillows under your knees to help you maintain this position comfortably. If it is physically difficult for you to touch your vulva, feel free to use a toy, a partner, or another solution so you can still look and explore.

   - Begin by looking at your genital area when you're not excited. Jot down a few notes to the following questions:

How many different parts can you see? Can you name them? Do you know what their function is physically and sexually?

Are you familiar with your normal aroma, and can you sense when it changes?

What words feel best for you to use when referring to your own genitals?

Are you experiencing any surprising or unexpected thoughts or feelings during this exercise?

For even more self-knowledge, do this exercise once a week for a month. If you have a regular menstrual cycle, see if your genitals change as your cycle progresses. See if it is possible to relax into the exercise and even enjoy your exploration. Write a few sentences describing your experience each week.

Week 1 Date: ____________

Reflections:

Week 2 Date: ______________

Reflections:

Week 3 Date: ______________

Reflections:

Week 4 Date: ______________

Reflections:

Giving Yourself Sexual Pleasure

The ability to give ourselves sexual pleasure is an important part of developing positive feelings about ourselves as sexual beings.

The reasons to masturbate are powerful: One, it feels good. And two, the more you know about how your body responds to different types of touch, the more you know what you like. This can help you to help your partner give you pleasure, but it is wonderful simply to know yourself.

There are other reasons to masturbate: It can provide a good release for vague anxieties, it can help you relax for sleep, it is good for your fantasy life, it is a good way to love yourself, and it is fun to see what happens.

We encourage you to reflect on what messages you have received about your own sexual exploration and what your beliefs and values are now.

5. Fill in the chart below to map out some of the messages you have received about masturbation throughout your life.

Message	Source	My age at the time
EXAMPLES:		
"It's perverted to do that."	*Friend at school*	*11 or 12*
"It's dirty."	*Mom*	*Not sure*
"It's normal; everyone does it."	*College roommate*	*18*

6. What are your beliefs about masturbation now?

   Do you feel happy with your sexual relationship with your own body?

   What might make it easier for you to give yourself sexual pleasure?

Somatic Practice: Shake It Out

In this chapter, we've spent a lot of time thinking about, looking at, and touching our own body. The following practice may be a welcome break from the intense sensations that can arise during focused activity.

Stand in a relaxed position. You may want to hold on to the back of a chair or table for balance. This activity can also be performed seated if standing is not a comfortable option.

Begin by paying some attention to your breathing. See if you can breathe just a little bit deeper than you would normally, and exhale without forcing air out.

Hold one hand out in front of your body and shake your arm gently. Try to relax your wrist and elbow. Imagine creating space inside those joints and letting them be loose. Do the same with your other arm.

Now lift one foot off the floor and shake out your leg. Try to relax your ankle, knee, and hip, so the movement is happening to your whole leg. Do the same with your other leg.

After gently shaking out your arms and legs, you can add gentle shaking movements to your hips, neck, and shoulders. Let your whole body experience some of this releasing movement.

PART

2

Actions: The Outer Journey

Just as the inner journey of early recovery requires us to be honest about our thoughts and feelings, the outer journey requires us to look honestly at the patterns of our behavior. Here we focus on our relationships and sexual interactions.

We need to take this process step by step, recognizing that self-care during this process is recovery in action.

CHAPTER 5

Exploring Sexual Behavior Patterns

I wish for you a grand and glorious opening—
an unbinding of old fears and judgments, a
softening into sexual joy, curiosity, and abundance.
May you bask in the sun and welcome light into any
hidden places. May you honor the dark and learn
from its mysteries. May laughter ripple through
your sex play, and may you awaken fully to the
wonder of your own succulent, wild self.

SARK, author of *Succulent Wild Woman: Dancing with Your Wonder-full Self!* 25th Anniversary Edition, personal interview

The outer journey of sexual recovery involves looking at our lives from a fresh perspective. Now the inner work we have done bears real fruit: We can see more clearly and be more honest with ourselves about what we see. Our understanding of our past actions and present interactions continues to deepen as our recovery unfolds. As inauthenticity melts away, we begin to understand the motivations behind our past actions and see what we can do today to nurture sexual growth and expansion.

In this chapter, we will take the time to look at our past experiences with clarity and compassion. We will identify patterns and behaviors we would like to leave in the past and those we would like to nurture and carry forward.

Emerging Patterns

Looking honestly at your sexual past is essential to sexual recovery. When you can see the patterns in your sexual relationships, you can begin to understand them, and then you can change them if you choose.

> ***Ash***
>
> *During their first experience with sobriety, Ash avoided talking about their sexual past. Ash had great difficulty accepting that there was a pattern of abuse in their relationships. They had taken great pains to construct a self-image of resilience and strength. Although they were aware that they had been sexually abused as a child, they had never considered subsequent sexual experiences as abuse, because they usually were getting basic survival needs met via sex: housing, drugs, physical safety, and so on.*
>
> *Working with a trauma therapist, Ash found that talking about their sexual patterns brought up painful material that had been buried for many years, including memories of sexual abuse by adults other than their stepfather. "I thought that when I was younger, I was using people to survive," Ash recalled. "But they were abusing me—I was a minor!" This was an important distinction for Ash to make.*
>
> *At the same time, when Ash reflected on their behavior as an adult, they could see how they had continued a pattern of having sex as a means to an end. "I did end up using some people, and hurting them. And some of them ended up hurting me too."*
>
> *Ash had used alcohol and drugs since adolescence to cope with the pain of trauma in their life and to drum up confidence in terrifying situations. Now that Ash was sober, the grief they felt about those relationships was overwhelming.*
>
> *"I don't want to go over every detail of who did what to whom," Ash remembers telling their AA sponsor. "I want to acknowledge that I caused a lot of harm, and that a lot of harm was done to me, and sometimes those things were happening at the same time. I don't want to make another list of wrongs."*
>
> *Ash's sponsor saw the wisdom in this choice, even though it went counter to Twelve Step traditions. For Ash, the catalog was less important than the acknowledgment that they had not always been in control and the reasons why. Ash needed to process their original sense of betrayal and fear stemming from childhood sexual abuse and abandonment, and so that was where they put their energy.*

Acknowledging your sexual history can be emotionally challenging. Your history may not stem from childhood sexual abuse like Ash's did, but everyone has a history that leads us to think, feel, and act the way we do now.

We believe that acknowledging your past, to the extent that you can, will help you move on to a healthier future. It requires a measure of faith in the process and in the resilience of your inner self. The following sections will guide you through acknowledging your past, recognizing patterns, and making clear choices about what you want to bring forward in your life and what you don't.

1. How do you feel about the prospect of looking honestly at your sexual past?

2. Make a list of supportive resources you can access if looking at your past becomes emotionally overwhelming.

   Examples:
   Make appointment with therapist to do this activity with them instead of alone.
   Call a close friend.
   Take this activity to my support group.

Childhood and Family Sexual Issues

The first task of the outer journey is to seek out the truth of your early childhood experiences. You can bring those messages out of your unconscious, make them explicit, look at your beliefs about sexuality, and recognize where you got them.

Answer the following questions with the first memories that come to mind.

3. How did your parents or caregivers express their feelings toward each other? Were they affectionate in front of you?

   Did your parents or caregivers speak openly with you about the changes you would experience in adolescence, or about sexual boundaries, safer sex, or pregnancy prevention?

   Was there ever a conversation about queer sexuality, or were you expected to be heterosexual?

If you had a complex family system with divorce or multiple parents and step-parents, did you notice a different culture about sexuality in different households?

What didn't your parents or caregivers say about sex, gender, or sexuality?

If you had contact with grandparents, did their values seem similar to or different from your parents' or caregivers' values?

Did you receive contradictory messages about sex, gender, and sexuality? What do you remember about this?

It is important to take a good look at the physical, emotional, and sexual boundaries in your childhood. Boundaries are about limits and protection; we need boundaries to define us and prevent our merging with others in sacrifice of our self. Boundaries do not control others; they tell others what we are experiencing, what we are going to do, and what we will not do.

4. Read the following statements, then check the one that feels *most true* for you.
   - ☐ I grew up with a healthy sense of boundaries—I was allowed age-appropriate privacy, felt free to talk with my parents/caregivers about my concerns, and did not have to take care of the adults in my life.
   - ☐ The adults who cared for me created a confusing or chaotic sense of boundaries. Sometimes boundaries were rigid, sometimes nonexistent.
   - ☐ I'm not sure I can identify how boundaries functioned in my childhood.

Why did you choose the statement you did? Is there anything you would add to this statement to make it more true for you?

5. Boundaries can serve to create both safety and opportunities for intimacy. Fill in the steps below to document how you were able to set a boundary in the present. This boundary does not need to be with an intimate partner—you can practice with anyone.

a. Notice that you need a boundary and identify what it is.

Example:

My co-worker likes to come up behind me and rub my shoulders. I don't like it. I need to make it clear that I don't want her to do this.

b. If appropriate, communicate your boundary to those who may be affected.

Example:

I was able to turn in my chair and say "no, thank you" when she tried to rub my shoulders this week.

c. Offer care to yourself, regardless of others' response to the boundary.

Example:

I felt so shaky after I said no. I texted my friend, who encouraged me. My co-worker seemed a little put off, but she accepted that I said no. I got myself a smoothie on the way home and enjoyed the cold sensation.

d. Take time to consider the boundary, and revise when appropriate for you.

Example:

I don't think I'll ever want my shoulders rubbed like that. I don't want to be touched from behind by someone I don't know well. Maybe it would be okay for a close friend to do it.

Naming the Personal Past

Naming your sexual experiences is crucial to developing honesty about sexuality in recovery. Saying aloud what happened and what didn't happen and naming it appropriately is often a painful process. We must grieve the hurts that have happened to us, and we also must grieve the harm we may have caused others.

It's very important to be able to see something as it really is and to label it according to the words that feel true for you.

We do not need to think of sexual violation in a hierarchy of "not so bad" to "really bad." Our experience of our own lives is usually more complex than that. Sometimes many years of "not so bad" experiences add up to a lot of harm, or one single "really bad" experience can affect years of your life.

Like many who have been harmed, you may have survived by shutting out the awareness of the reality of your sexual experiences. You may have replicated harmful behaviors too. As you grow in recovery, you will find that moving beyond old behaviors means telling the truth about where you have been.

6. Take the time to name some of your personal past. What language feels true for you to use for your experiences? How does it feel to name these experiences?

Joining a Support Group

Naming your past may be easiest to do while in a recovery group that includes sexuality as an issue. In such a group, many women, nonbinary people, and gender-expansive people feel safe for the first time in their lives to talk about and name what actually happened. You may discover that your experiences with sexuality are similar to others' experiences and that other people in your group know and understand exactly what you are talking about.

7. If you are already part of a therapeutic support or recovery group, you can describe the group below. If you are not part of a group, imagine a group that might feel safe and encouraging for you to be in as you work through this material.

   Who is in the group?

   What gets talked about in the group?

   What do the group members do to help you feel welcomed and safe to share?

   Who leads the meetings?

   What insights have you gained (would like to gain) from participating in this group?

Most recovery programs have directories of meetings and groups, and you can often find offshoots by asking around in those communities. Many therapists have groups they can recommend, and a large number of counselors run groups that have information posted online. You may need to search for a little while to find the right group. There are a few suggestions for places to begin in the Resources section. We strongly encourage you to consider the benefits of community support as you continue your sexual recovery.

Somatic Practice: Painting Your Bubble

This somatic practice begins in a standing position. If you cannot easily stand for a few minutes at a time, feel free to do the practice seated. If practicing in a group, make sure everyone has enough space around them for their arms to be fully extended in every direction.

Begin by closing or lowering your eyes for a moment and noticing a few breaths as they flow in and out. Feel your feet on the ground.

With eyes open or closed, imagine there is a beautiful, colored light emanating from your fingertips. Whatever color you imagine is the right one for you today.

Very slowly, begin to move your arms up and down, extending up, out, and all around you, moving your hands gently as if your fingers were the bristles of a large paintbrush. Imagine that you are creating the inside of a large bubble around your body, made of this colorful light. You can see out, and others can see in.

Turn your body around as it is comfortable for you, to complete making the bubble shape all around you with your gentle arm movements. Continue bringing your hands up and down around you until you imagine the bubble of light around you is complete.

This bubble is your space. You get to decide who and what comes in.

Take a few breaths and enjoy the beauty of the color you have imagined.

If you are doing this practice in a group, each participant can share what color their bubble was—sometimes they are quite surprising!

CHAPTER 6

Facing Our Challenges

When my body feels good, my life feels good, and I want to keep going, and fight for my right to exist and love and grow and evolve. This is true whether it is in the context of a meeting, or a relationship, or a night of lovemaking. That doesn't mean the absence of discomfort or awkwardness or hard conversations or learning. But the majority of experience should be presence—being fully alive. And I think that comes from experiencing ease, pleasure, connection. As Nina [Simone] sang: "Feelin' good."

adrienne maree brown, *Pleasure Activism: The Politics of Feeling Good*

We are rich, complex beings, and for many of us, sexuality is a central facet of this richness. It does not exist in isolation, apart from the rest of life. Our sexuality is affected by everything that affects our mood: stress, anxiety, cravings, sleep, nutrition, social connections, and so on. We can benefit from considering how our sexual feelings may relate to what else is going on in our lives. Recognizing these connections can open up a new level of self-understanding.

In this chapter, we will spend some time with a few of the most common challenges we see in the sexual lives of women, nonbinary people, and gender-diverse people who are in recovery from addiction and trauma. These include imbalanced relationship dynamics, sex avoidance, and out-of-control sexual behavior. If you see yourself in these descriptions, you are in great company—the company of people in their own recovery process.

Healthy sexuality, as you define it for yourself, begins with honest awareness of your past actions and identification of the values and desires you hold in the present. Then you practice bringing your behavior into alignment with your values and desires.

Power Imbalance in Relationships

Women in our society are socialized to be in imbalanced relationships; that is, we are taught to feel satisfaction and fulfillment from meeting the needs of others, from putting others first in our lives. We come from many generations of women who learned to center their lives around the needs of partners, spouses, children, or aging parents, often at the expense of their own growth, development, and satisfaction. This story is more complex for trans women, nonbinary people, and gender-expansive people, and women who partner with other women. However, no one is untouched by the dominant gender norms in our society.

Power imbalance can be a part of sexual play, as in kink or BDSM. While traditionally seen as an acronym for *bondage, discipline, dominance, submission, sadism, and masochism*, BDSM refers to a wide range of relational and sexual practices that usually involve a clear power exchange among partners. In consensual kink, not quite synonymous with BDSM, there may or may not be a power imbalance as part of the experience. *Consensual kink* refers more broadly to sexual practices that fall outside dominant norms. For both kink and BDSM, however, a power dynamic is a conscious choice made by all involved, and among the many feelings it can elicit, satisfaction and pleasure should appear.

In contrast, the power imbalances we will think about here tend to be built over time without discussion, cause significant distress, and create conflict in relationships that make sexual connection difficult to achieve.

1. Take a moment to write out what the following words mean to you when thinking about sexual relationships:

   Power

Mutuality

Dignity

Respect

Safety

Michelle and Chris

Michelle and her husband, Chris, arrived at a surprising impasse while working through their disconnection in therapy: They both felt that the other person relied on them for too much emotional and physical labor in their family home. Michelle had identified that her drinking, in addition to other ways it offered her relief, was a way to escape the pressures of motherhood, especially the exhaustion and frustration of being a stay-at-home mom. She felt that Chris expected her to do everything perfectly like a 1950s housewife, and she was angry with him for not helping more around the house. She felt that he had more power in the relationship than she did.

For Chris, Michelle had seemed incapable of caring for their home or children the instant he arrived home from work, because she was drinking so heavily. He felt responsible for the safety of their children, caring for them when Michelle was drunk at night, when she was out at boozy brunch, or when she was hungover, and then monitoring her for poor decisions when she was alone with their children, even while he was at work.

When Michelle quit drinking and began her recovery, she still needed hours away from the children to go to meetings. Even though Chris saw improvement in their home life and was glad Michelle was sober, their relationship still needed deeper communication about their expectations of each other and how they could support each other going forward so their relationship would feel more balanced for both of them.

2. Have you been involved in an imbalanced relationship, where one partner wielded more power than the other in a way that caused you distress?

Have you felt like the more or less powerful partner in a relationship? How did this affect you?

Sex Avoidance

We may feel the need to avoid sex with others for many reasons. Most of them boil down to our sense of safety. If we are not safe to express our sexuality, we will try not to. If our body sends danger signals when someone touches us, we will avoid contact. Sometimes we work on creating more safety for ourselves through sobriety, recovery, therapy, and group support, but we still feel fearful, ambivalent, or avoidant of sexual experiences.

Sex avoidance for a period of time may be called *celibacy* or *abstinence*. There is nothing wrong with taking some time to evaluate your own sexual feelings without engaging in sex with others.

What is important to notice is *how it feels* to release the expectation of sex. If avoiding sex feels good to you, like a weight off your shoulders, then refraining from sexual contact with others may be an experiment in self-awareness and recovery.

However, if avoiding sex feels distressing to you, then you may want to spend some more time investigating the nature of your avoidance.

The emotional quality of the avoidance matters. Some people are not fearful; they avoid sex because it simply isn't what they want for themselves. Some wish to be more sexually connected but experience symptoms of trauma when they try: dissociation, freezing, numbing, and so on. If you know you are avoiding sexual contact but aren't sure why, use the exercises below to gain some insight.

3. Rate the statements below on a scale of 0 (strongly disagree) to 5 (strongly agree):

   When I am sexually excited, I often also feel a strong negative emotion, such as fear, anxiety, pressure, or insecurity.

   0 1 2 3 4 5

   It is difficult for me to stay present during sex. My mind often goes elsewhere.

   0 1 2 3 4 5

   Sometimes when I am touched a certain way, I freeze up.

   0 1 2 3 4 5

   I used to feel strong attraction to potential/actual partners, but I rarely feel that way anymore.

   0 1 2 3 4 5

I think I may need to make some changes in how I have sex/with whom I have sex.

0 1 2 3 4 5

I do not have a lot of experience with sex without substance use.

0 1 2 3 4 5

I need to be really close to someone to be able to be sexual with them.

0 1 2 3 4 5

I prefer to be sexual with people I don't know well.

0 1 2 3 4 5

I feel confident expressing my sexual preferences and desires with my partner.

0 1 2 3 4 5

I feel there is still a lot I don't know about my own sexual body and sexual preferences.

0 1 2 3 4 5

Reading through your answers to the above, what thoughts and feelings arise in you?

Out-of-Control Sexual Behavior (OCSB)

Sexual avoidance and out-of-control sexual behavior may seem like opposites, but they are both coping mechanisms for pain in our sexual lives. Women, nonbinary people, and gender-expansive people who have experienced sexual abuse or rape are very likely to choose one extreme or the other as a way to cope with trauma and feel some control over what happens to them. Therapist and author Douglas Braun-Harvey defines *out-of-control sexual behavior* (OCSB) as "a sexual health problem in which consensual sexual urges, thoughts, or behaviors feel out of control."[1]

Note that this does not include sexual assault or rape that happens to a person while they are intoxicated, nor sexual assault or rape that a person may commit while intoxicated. OCSB refers to engaging in sexual behaviors that violate our sexual values, within a framework of consensual experiences. In other words, while our behavior may hurt someone's feelings or cause us distress, the behaviors are not crimes against another person.

There is no specific definition for what an "out of control" behavior is—for one person, having more than twenty partners in a year may feel out of control, while for another, that feels perfectly normal. Aside from the basics of mutual consent, you are the only one who knows what your values are, and when you are in violation of them.

4. Take some time to write three to five sentences in response to each of the following questions:

   What do I want when I want sex?

What kind of sexual partner(s) do I want to have?

What level of sexual risk am I comfortable with?

Would my former partners say I was interested in their boundaries and got appropriate consent from them for our sexual experiences?

Would I say my former partners have been interested in my boundaries and got consent from me for our sexual experiences?

The Sexual History Lifeline

Filling out a Sexual History Lifeline is an effective way to see how your sexual behavior has been shaped by your life experiences, including your addictions or compulsive behaviors. Figure 2 is an example, reflecting Ash's experiences. Once you understand the exercise, you will complete your own.

The Sexual History Lifeline starts with the bottom horizontal line: from zero to the age you are now, in five-year increments. Along the side, a vertical line starts at -10, counts up to zero, and then continues up to 10. This is the measure of whether an experience was positive or negative for you. As you draw your sexual history over the years into this chart, you can label any experiences that are especially meaningful.

After you have charted your sexual history, you can add another line (dotted or in another color) that charts your history with problematic substance use, disordered eating, other self-harming behavior, or significant trauma symptoms.

In the case of substances or addictive behaviors, it may be challenging to decide how "positive" or "negative" an experience was, given the confusing way our substances and addictive behaviors make us feel better in the short term. Use your best judgment in the present. In general, you may assume that times of out-of-control use would be shown as dipping low on the chart.

FIGURE 2

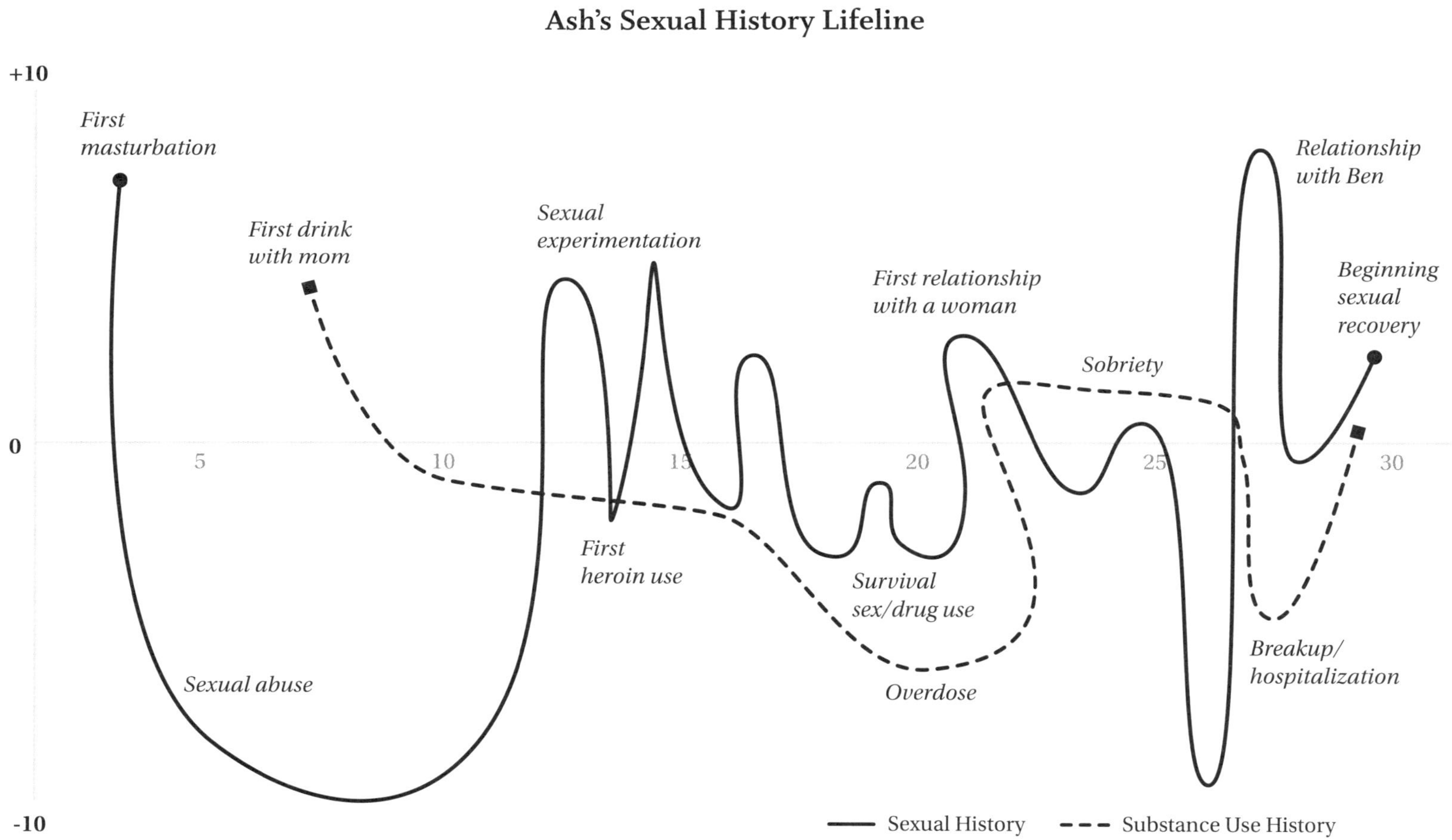
Ash's Sexual History Lifeline
+10
0
-10
5
10
15
20
25
30
First masturbation
First drink with mom
Sexual experimentation
First heroin use
Sexual abuse
First relationship with a woman
Survival sex/drug use
Overdose
Sobriety
Relationship with Ben
Beginning sexual recovery
Breakup/ hospitalization
Sexual History
Substance Use History

Explanation of Ash's Sexual History Lifeline

Figure 2 shows Ash's Sexual History Lifeline. Ash has drawn a line with the years of their life marked off at five-year intervals. The space above the line has been designated for pleasant experiences (marked from 1 to 10) and the space below has been designated for painful ones (marked from -1 to -10). Ash has indicated their sexual experiences with a solid line and their alcohol/drug experiences with a dotted line.

Ash begins by charting their sexual history with a solid line. Ash remembers masturbating at age three. It is a positive, pleasurable experience, guilt-free because they didn't yet have a name for what they were doing.

By age four, Ash was experiencing sexual abuse from their stepfather, which included a violent rape at age ten. During this time, Ash dissociated from their body to self-protect.

From ages ten to fifteen, Ash engaged in constant experimental sexual behavior. Some was enjoyable, but some was scary or uncomfortable. Around this time, their self-esteem began to be connected to being attractive to boys, even though they didn't feel like a feminine girl.

Between the ages of fifteen and eighteen, Ash had a variety of sexual experiences, often with older boys or men in some positions of power, like the staff member at their group home. Once they were out of the group home, Ash continued to have sex to get basic needs met. They are not sure how many partners they had during this time. They lived with a group of other queer youth who were sharing a motel room, using drugs, and trading sex to get by.

At twenty-three, Ash spent three months in jail, got sober in a rehabilitation stay, and came out as nonbinary. They briefly entered a relationship with a woman. This was a mostly positive experience for Ash, even though they prefer to date and have sex with men.

For the next four years, Ash moved in and out of recovery and return to use. They worked many different jobs and dated new people but struggled to enjoy being sexual while sober. At twenty-six, Ash experienced sexual violence that triggered a difficult depression.

At twenty-seven, Ash met Ben. The relationship was fun, respectful, supportive, and sexy for a year before Ash began experiencing panic attacks and nightmares.

During a psychiatric emergency, Ash was hospitalized and then released without a coherent treatment plan. Ash returned to using familiar substances. Ben broke off the relationship. Ash has not had a sexual partner since that breakup. However, their sexual recovery has progressed. Ash is now able to masturbate without triggering a fear response in their body, so their line is turning upward.

Next, Ash charts their relationship to substance use with a dotted line. They remember their first sip of beer and drag off a cigarette at age six. This is one of the few memories they have with their mother, who died before they were out of foster care.

Ash recalls drinking their mother and stepfather's alcohol in secret at age eight, and then trying to get older men to buy them alcohol after school once they were in foster care.

Ash's first experience with heroin happened at age sixteen, with a boy from school who had stolen it from his sibling. Ash knew it was the drug their mother used and was curious to see why she would choose the drug over her own children. What began as casual use became more serious over the years.

By eighteen, Ash was using heroin and alcohol daily. Their use had ebbs and flows, depending on their financial situation or their health. They had a terrifying experience of overdose at twenty-one, but a friend used naloxone to revive them, and Ash tapered down their use for about a year.

When they were arrested for driving under the influence and without a license, Ash wasn't at the peak of their heroin use, and they were getting tired of the way their life was going. During their three months in jail, they received support from other sober women. They sought treatment. During that transformational time, Ash became ready to say publicly that they were a nonbinary person. They wanted to use they/them pronouns and be referred to by the name *Ash* instead of their legal name. Ash had trouble plotting this period on the chart as either positive or negative, because while it was terrible to be locked up and scary to seek treatment, it was also an important time for their sobriety and self-identity.

At twenty-four, Ash had been in recovery for a year and was stuck on the Fourth Step because they hadn't spoken with their sponsor about their history of sexual abuse. They dropped out of Alcoholics Anonymous and had some fluctuation in their use. During a period of sobriety at twenty-seven, they met Ben.

After their psychiatric emergency and hospitalization, Ash returned to use. When Ben broke up with them, Ash became homeless again. Finally, they returned to recovery with a renewed sense of dedication.

After three years of sobriety, Ash became a peer counselor to others struggling with addiction. Ash also started working with a trauma therapist to specifically address their history of sexual abuse, unwanted sex, and out-of-control sexual behavior. They have not yet begun a new sexual relationship with anyone, but they are starting to feel more capable of communicating about their sexual feelings and desires.

5. Now you can fill in the blank Sexual History Lifeline according to your own experiences.

FIGURE 3

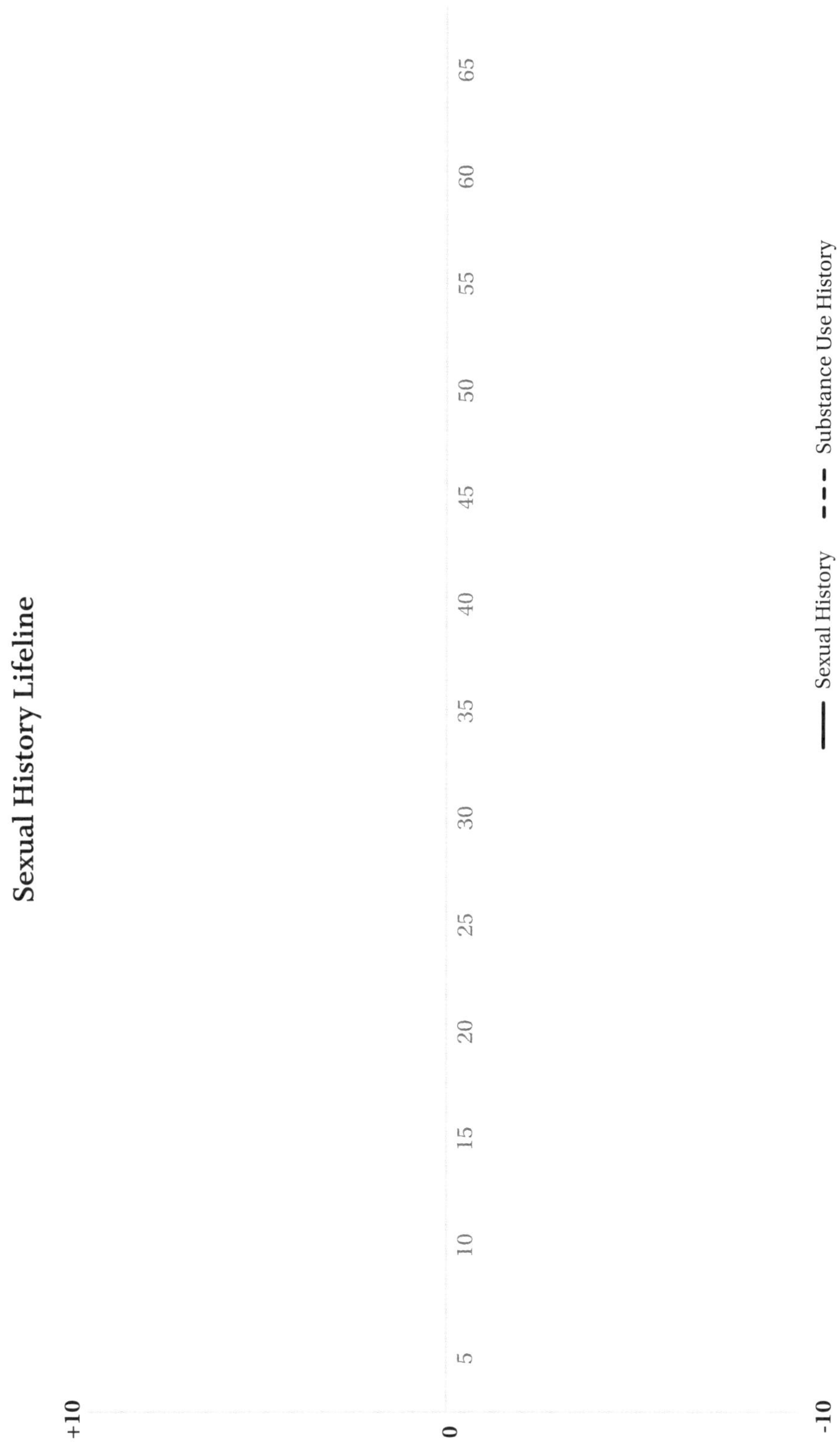

Sexual History Lifeline
+10
0
-10
5
10
15
20
25
30
35
40
45
50
55
60
65
Sexual History
Substance Use History

6. Take a few moments to look at your own Sexual History Lifeline. You can answer the questions below or write down any reflections that come to you.

   Do you see any patterns in the Sexual History Lifeline you made? How would you describe them?

   Is there anything in your Sexual History Lifeline that you're surprised to see?

   How do your sexual experiences and your history with addiction/compulsive behaviors/trauma symptoms/self-destructive actions interact?

What other reflections do you have about this exercise?

When you look back through your past to identify your sexual experiences, you may remember incidents that you had forgotten, or you may be surprised at how poignant many of your memories are. You may also become aware of certain patterns, especially in the way your sexual history and your history with addiction or compulsive behaviors interact. Seeing how the lines intertwine, the ways they affect and reflect each other, can provide insight into how your sexual behavior and substance use or other out-of-control behaviors have accompanied you in your life. Understanding this connection greatly enhances your chance to create the kind of sexual life you want in recovery.

Somatic Practice: Rowing Forward

Rowing forward is a physical movement practice that can be performed standing or seated. If standing, place one foot slightly ahead of the other. Imagine you are standing in a small (but steady!) boat, holding on to oars in both hands. Make loose fists with your hands to simulate holding on to an oar, and hold your hands out in front of you at waist height.

Begin to move your hands as if you are rowing the boat forward in the water, allowing your body to move gently with the motion. Don't worry about getting exactly the right motion; just do a motion that is comfortable to you that gives you a slight sensation of forward movement.

As you row forward, breathe in and out slowly and evenly.

You are moving forward in your life. You get to decide what comes with you.

You can imagine rowing away from painful experiences or rowing past scenes from your life that you would like to let go. Keep your arms moving gently and remind yourself that the past is behind you, and you are moving forward. You can revisit your past anytime you like, but for right now, you are focusing on the sensation of moving into your own future, where you get to make conscious choices that reflect who you are.

After about a minute of rowing, allow your arms to relax at your sides. Close or lower your eyes, take a deep breath, and let it out slowly. Allow whatever sensations, thoughts, or feelings that arise in you to come and go.

CHAPTER 7

How We Chose Our Partners

SHOULD YOU SEND THAT TEXT

Don't ask me. I'm terrible at it.
Last week I posed the same
question to a friend, who said

"There is nothing in it for you."
But I am in it. "Okay," she said.
"Set an alarm for two weeks

and then see how you feel."
Great advice, I said. I waited
two hours. All my alarms

were going off. So I sent it
and felt victorious and hid
under the bed next to

a dog toy, some dust and
what do you think? Is it love?

Jillian Weise (aka Cy), *Cyborg Detective*

Whether we do it consciously or unconsciously, by actively seeking or passively accepting, we do choose our sexual relationship partners. Looking at the behaviors of people we have chosen over the course of our lives can be very revealing.

It can be painful to investigate the past and see all the justifications we made for behavior that was uncomfortable for us. At other times, we may have been seeking healthy, safe partners with whom we could find refuge.

If you are currently in a relationship, you may fear that looking honestly at your partner would require you to change the relationship. Before you choose to avoid looking honestly at your current partner, though, realize that honesty doesn't mean you have to make immediate changes. It simply requires you to tell the truth about what's happening now. Telling the truth allows you to assess your options, to see that there are choices. Then you can make the decisions that will help you to take care of yourself.

If you are not in a relationship right now but are actively dating or would like to be in a relationship in the future, this chapter can help you identify those patterns you do not wish to repeat, consider what behaviors you need to be aware of, and identify what feels good to you in a partnership.

If you are nonmonogamous, partner selection may require even more consideration, as your relationships will all be mutually affected by the health and quality of each.

If you are not in and do not plan to be in a relationship, taking a look at your past can still inform you about your beliefs and habits.

Regardless of your relationship status, looking at how you have chosen to be in relationship will help you make clearer, more grounded choices going forward.

The Ideal Lover vs. Reality

While swiping on dating apps, introducing ourselves in meetings, or scanning whatever room we are in, we often look for those who seem to fit our image of the ideal lover. Many dating coaches will encourage single people to make a list of traits they are looking for in a partner, as well as a list of deal-breakers. We carry our lists inside us and measure new people up.

As we come to know the people we date better and better, they become real individuals to us, so that we can no longer project our ideal onto them. Eventually, we either move on or choose to build a more conscious relationship. Remember that all people are contradictory and complex, including you!

1. Take a moment to identify one or more significant romantic/sexual relationships from your past. If you have not had a significant relationship, you can think about someone you were interested in, or you can think about the relationships that were modeled for you as a younger person in your family and community.

List the person or people below:

Did this person/any of these people exhibit any of the following traits during your relationship? Check all that apply.

- ☐ Addiction/substance use issues, including alcohol
- ☐ Emotionally unavailable or distant
- ☐ Physically abusive behavior
- ☐ Emotionally abusive behavior (name-calling, yelling, insults, etc.)
- ☐ Stalking
- ☐ Dishonesty
- ☐ Sexual infidelity

There are many ways to describe and define abuse, abandonment, and other painful relationship issues. While it can be helpful to read a list of some behaviors that "qualify" as abuse, we encourage you to take the next step.

Look inward to *define for yourself* what behaviors have made you feel demeaned, diminished, disrespected, and harmed.

List them here.

Examples:

When my boyfriend drove the car too fast, to scare me.

My girlfriend never returns my calls but gets angry if I don't pick up the phone when she calls me.

If I made a mistake, my ex-husband would always make fun of me, then tell me I was "too sensitive" if I asked him to stop.

2. Identify a behavior from your list above that you do not want to tolerate again in your life. Complete a short contract in which you make a promise to yourself to uphold your boundary about this behavior.

Example:

I, *Michelle* (YOUR NAME), will not tolerate *yelling in anger* (THE BEHAVIOR) in my relationships.

If my partner does *yell in anger* (THE BEHAVIOR), I will remind them that this is a boundary for me and remove myself from the situation until I can be assured that the behavior has ceased.

I, ________ (YOUR NAME), will not tolerate ________ (THE BEHAVIOR) in my relationships.

If my partner does ________ (THE BEHAVIOR), I will remind them that this is a boundary for me and remove myself from the situation until I can be assured that the behavior has ceased.

If you are concerned that you are involved in an abusive relationship at the present time, we recommend using the hotlines listed here and getting in touch with an advocacy group. They will help you plan how to get support from your family, your friends, your place of worship, or other community resources. They provide practical advice for how to deal with the police and legal system, should you choose to pursue a restraining order or other legal options. Most of all, they can assist you in creating alternatives for yourself, such as finding places and people to sustain you during the process of extricating yourself from an abusive partner.

National Domestic Violence Hotline:
1-800-799-SAFE (7233) or 1-800-787-3224 (TTY)

Rape, Abuse & Incest National Network (RAINN)
Sexual Assault Hotline: 1-800-656-HOPE (4673)

3. Now let's list the qualities and characteristics you are looking for in a partner, or some positive qualities of your current partner:

    Examples:
    Good listener
    Wants to get to know my family
    Understands my past and doesn't judge

Sometimes, while thinking about our choice of partners, we will arrive at insights about our own behavior as well. Relationships that are not considered abusive can still be very painful for us when they change or end. How we handle our own feelings of hurt, anger, or abandonment are an important part of our relationship history.

Tamara

As her recovery progressed, Tamara began to understand that she had become the emotionally unavailable partner to her ex-wife, Alisha. Originally, Tamara felt blindsided by the divorce. She was hurt and angry and felt that Alisha had not tried hard enough to stay together. After a year of recovery from her addiction to painkillers, while using alternative forms of pain management and processing her emotions with a therapist, Tamara developed new insights.

She said, "When Alisha told me she wanted a divorce, I was stunned and went into a deep depression. I thought we had it all worked out. I knew we weren't madly and passionately in love anymore, but we had worked out a life, and I was proud of us being the only middle-aged Black lesbian couple in our small town! I worked long hours at the university, she had plenty of friends to spend time with after she came home from work, and she believed in my mission and purpose, so she never complained about how often I wasn't home. She worried about my health, but she never told me she was unhappy.

"Now I see that we simply lived our own lives and left each other alone. We never talked about anything more serious than what to have for dinner or who was bothering us at work. She definitely tried—I remember nights when she would open up conversations about having sex or having more romance, and I would shut her down. I was too caught up in my work and dealing with my pain from the accident. I thought she would wait for me to get better. I thought we had time to fix whatever she thought was a problem. I didn't realize that I had been withdrawing from her emotionally and sexually for years." Tamara withdrew from connection with Alisha, and while Alisha tried to pursue Tamara for a time, eventually it was too hurtful for her, and she decided she needed to end their marriage.

The Family Map

The family map is a diagram of the relationships that exist between you and your family members. You decide who belongs on the map—if you were raised by multiple people, in foster care, or in another nontraditional family structure, choose the people with whom you had the most contact.

The family map is a visual tool that represents the relationship patterns you were born into, and it can help you get information on your emotional history.

The center circle represents you, and the larger circle is where you will draw your map. Draw circles that represent each member of your family, or the people who were significant in your childhood. Use the key to draw lines between you and your family members that describe your current relationship with each person. If you'd like, you can also draw lines between the other circles to represent the relationships your family members have with each other.

Arati's family map offers an example to aid you in drawing and analyzing your own. After reading her example, you can complete your own family map.

FIGURE 4

Arati's Family Map

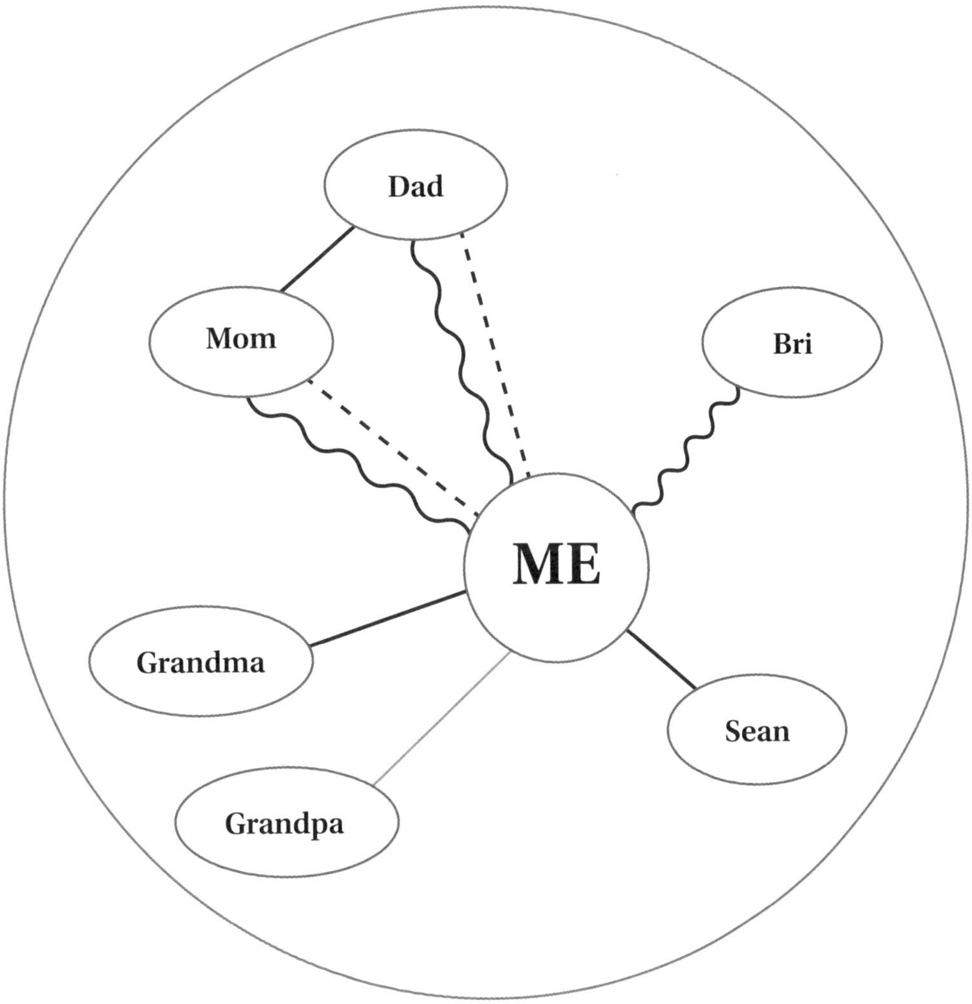

KEY
Strong
Weak
Confusing
Angry
Broken/No Connection

Explanation of Arati's Family Map

Arati drew her immediate family, including her mom; her dad; her sister, Bri; and her son, Sean. Although she had aunts and uncles who were close, she chose to keep her map simple at first. She used dotted and wavy lines to show that her relationships with her parents felt weak and confusing—weaker with her father, more confusing with her mother. Then she added a wavy line to connect to her sister as well. She drew a strong line of connection to her son. She added her grandparents to the map and drew a strong line of connection to her grandmother, with a slightly lighter line to her grandfather.

Looking at her map, Arati realized that before she had her son, she would have drawn a strong line of connection to her mother and father. She felt sad to recognize this change. When Arati imagined adding a new partner to this map, she envisioned someone who would be able to connect with both her son and her parents.

Arati also recognized that her relationship with her sister was not as close as it might be. They tended to rely on their parents for reasons to see each other, and both lived very busy lives. Bri did reach out regularly to check in on Arati's son, Sean, and Arati felt that trying to share more of her life with her sister could feel supportive. She wondered how her sister's map would look.

Arati perceived her parents' relationship to be very strong, so she drew a strong line of connection between them. However, she realized that she didn't really know what their connection was like with her sister, or with her grandparents. Her family was consistent in fulfilling obligations, marking holidays, and gathering together on special occasions, but that didn't give her the information she was looking for now. She also knew that their extended family would provide a lot more complexity to the map.

4. Now you can complete your own family map.

FIGURE 5

Family Map

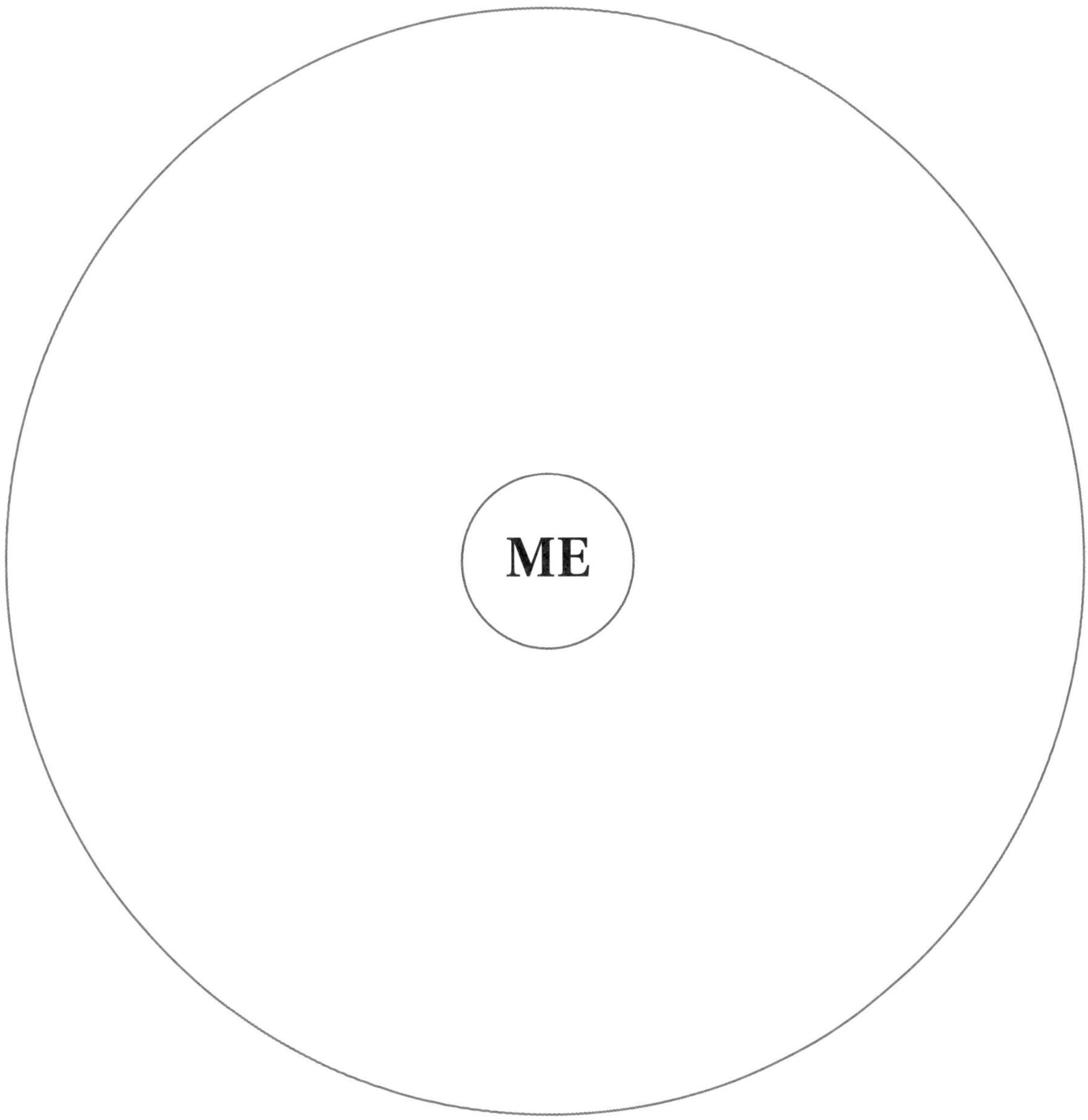

KEY

Strong · Weak · Confusing · Angry · Broken/No Connection

Reflect on the Family Map

5. What Arati took from this exercise was that deep emotional connection was not taught to her in her family as much as the values of fulfilling familial duty. Arati knew that she was going to have to create her own path to fulfilling relationships that didn't look like her parents' or grandparents'. By putting energy into her own recovery and expressing her sexuality, she was doing something she had not seen before in her own family.

   What reflections come to your mind when you look at your own family map?

The Relationship History Chart

The Relationship History Chart will give you a picture of who you are in a sexual relationship. This should illuminate how you have developed as a partner, and which patterns and traits you might be repeating. By studying the chart, you can get clues of what you need to do for sexual recovery. You will see the way you interact in relationships and the kinds of partners that you choose. Certain themes, feelings, and characteristics are bound to emerge as patterns. As you reflect on what you see, you will begin to have a deeper understanding of yourself.

Instructions for Completing the Relationship History Chart

6. Across the top of the chart are spaces for the names of people with whom you remember having sexual relationships. You will make the call about what qualifies as a "relationship." (We suggest that if you had feelings about a person, even if they didn't return the feelings, it is best to include them.)

   If there are sexual relationships you have trouble remembering because of your substance use or trauma symptoms, do not worry about trying to recall them. Work with the memories that are available to you. If you are currently in a relationship that has sexual expectations, even if you are avoiding sexual connection, put that person's name in the last (most recent) space.

   In the other cells of the chart, you will fill in:

   - **Characteristics of the person.** List the words that best describe the person emotionally. Paint a descriptive picture of the person. Examples of words to describe the person might include *cold*, *warm*, *indirect*, *present*, *distant*, *affectionate*, *mean*, *caring*, *gentle*, *loyal*, *insecure*, *honest*, *reliable*, *sarcastic*, or *courageous*.

   - **Characteristics of the relationship.** Use words that best describe your interaction with this person—that is, how the relationship felt to you. Examples might include *caring*, *distant*, *fun*, *sympathetic*, *hopeless*, *warm*, *supportive*, *intense*, *uncommunicative*, *boring*, *deceitful*, *mutual*, *indifferent*, *critical*, *exciting*, *stable*, or *toxic*.

   - **Addictive behaviors.** Describe any problematic use of alcohol or other substances by you or your partner during the relationship, as well as other addictive/compulsive behaviors either of you might have engaged in.

   - **Sexual qualities of the relationship.** Pick words that best describe the sexual qualities of the relationship. You might consider whether the relationship was *mutual*, *passionate*, *one-sided*, *open*, *nonexistent*, *compulsive*, *accepting*, *shameful*, *tender*, *affectionate*, *routine*, *dutiful*, *adventurous*, or *confusing*.

   - **Sexual likes and dislikes in the relationship.** Go through the sexual qualities of the relationship that you've just listed and sort them into two categories: those you liked and those you didn't. This is also the place to reflect on the sexual activities you engaged in and whether you generally liked or disliked them.

FIGURE 6

Relationship History Chart

Name	1)	2)	3)	4)	5)
Characteristics of the person					
Characteristics of the relationship					
Addictive behaviors					
Sexual qualities of the relationship					
Sexual likes and dislikes in the relationship					

7. When looking at your Relationship History Chart, do you see any patterns in your relationships? Describe them here.

How much of your sexual life has been determined by your partner's desires and preferences versus your own?

What were the qualities and characteristics of the sexual partnerships that brought you the most sexual satisfaction?

Living in the Present

Living in the present means that you are consciously aware of what is going on for you right now. You may say, "But of course I'm living in the present! Where else is there to live?" The fact is, however, that we spend most of our time either in the past, feeling uncomfortable about things we've already done, or in the future, worrying about, planning for, or trying to control events that haven't yet happened.

When we spend our time in the past, we carry our history around with us. We are burdened with expectations based on things that have happened to us, and we expect that these things will continue to happen to us. But no matter how much of your life you've spent elsewhere, you can learn to live in the present, and you can reclaim your past without having to reexperience it. When you live in the present, you will reconnect with more of yourself.

Perhaps the best way to learn to live in the present is to allow your loving observer self into your consciousness. The *observer self* is a phrase used by mindfulness teachers and therapists to acknowledge a nonjudgmental part of you who acts as a witness to the events of your life. The observer self can look at how you feel and act and know that particular actions and feelings are not your total self.

The observer self is a mirror in which you can look at your own behaviors and actions without judgment. Your observer self provides you with a quiet place from which to view your own behavior with reflection and acceptance. Your observer self loves you unconditionally, no matter what. Your observer self is rooting for you.

8. Write a letter to you from your observer self. The tone of this letter should be loving and encouraging—your observer self does not judge, criticize, or insult you in any way. Imagine your observer self earnestly communicating love to you, and let the words pour out. You can also draw pictures and rename your observer self if you wish.

   Dear ______________________________,

   With love, Your Observer Self

9. Pick one of the following prompts and write whatever comes to your mind. You can set a timer for five minutes or simply write until you reach the end of the page. If you enjoy the practice, pick a new prompt for each day and see what has changed for you by the end of a week. These prompts can be used again and again to create a daily inventory.

- Did I feel sexual/attracted to/interested in sexuality today? How did I express this?
- What felt good to me today? (Describe it using as many of your five senses as you can.)
- Who helped me feel a safe connection today? If no one comes to mind, whom might I be able to ask for some connection tomorrow? What is it about this person that helps me feel connected to them?
- What pattern from my childhood showed up today? How do I feel about this?
- How safe do I feel in my own body today? What might help me feel more relaxed and safe in my body?
- What can I feel proud of today?
- What is a sexual experience I would like to have, or a fantasy that I'm thinking about?

Partner selection involves choices. Understanding the influence of our past relationships is the first step. Seeing how and where they continue to affect us is the second. Realizing that we have choices about whom to select in the present and future is part of the awakening experience. It is important to acknowledge to yourself that completing the exercises in this chapter is a major step in being honest about your sexual past. Give yourself credit for being willing to take that step!

Somatic Practice: Self-Hugging

While self-hugging can be practiced anytime, an especially powerful time is first thing upon waking up or after a stressful experience.

Self-hugging is exactly what it sounds like. Wrap your arms around yourself and squeeze. If you like, you can lean your head into the hug as well, the way you would if you felt totally safe with someone. As a bonus, you can say kind words to yourself in your mind or out loud. What would someone who loves you say to you right now? "I got you," or "You're okay, I'm here with you," or "Let's have a great day"?

If it is physically challenging for you to move your arms this way, you can squeeze or press on your own hands or forearms with the same intention.

Take a full breath and a long exhale while you hug yourself. Repeat two to three more times before you release.

PART

3

The Power of Choice: Ongoing Recovery

The transition between early and ongoing recovery is marked by a feeling of reconnection with your loving observer self, that wise and nonjudgmental part of yourself from whom you have been estranged for so long. As you move into ongoing recovery, a stage that you will explore for the rest of your life, this connection with your loving observer self allows you to tackle deeper issues that were too overwhelming to handle earlier.

Many people find that their relationship issues rise to the surface after some period of recovery. This can be discouraging at first, but ultimately it is a sign that you are becoming more aware of how you feel and what you want. The issues can become clear because some space has been made for them. This is uncomfortable, but it does not mean you are doing anything wrong. On the contrary, you are in a new place, with new challenges.

In ongoing recovery, you will move toward healing the pain of any prior sexual abuse and dissolving your shame. When you are able to recognize and move through painful memories and feelings, you will discover your core of power.

Building a foundation of honesty is an essential element in early recovery. As you continue to build on this foundation in ongoing recovery, you will begin the major task of reclaiming your sense of empowerment. This will allow you to create a healthy, fulfilling sexual life, on your own terms.

CHAPTER 8

Choosing a New Sexual Life

It is hard to describe to someone who has not experienced it, what it is for a body to open, but it is just as holy as falling before the pulpit and as righteous as a riot. It is the breaking of what binds. It is undoing so that we can become.

Prentis Hemphill, *What It Takes to Heal: How Transforming Ourselves Can Change the World*

The journey of sexual recovery is developmental. You must walk down the path of early recovery before you can turn the corner into ongoing recovery. Yet each person creates their own unique version of that path, tackling these stages in their own way, doing inner work or taking outer actions as the need arises and issues present themselves.

Remember that the process of sexual awakening and recovering can take the form of an upward spiral (see Figure 1 on page 41). As you pass through one stage, and then another and another, you will revisit the same issues but on higher levels of understanding and work. Where first you needed the most basic definitions, now you also see the subtleties. Life seems to present the same issues over and over again. But when you are working on your recovery, you will see these issues with a new sense of depth and complexity.

Progress means moving to another level of self-exploration, not "fixing" yourself or getting rid of a particular issue once and for all. A familiar situation arises, and rather than do what you've always done, you see more than one way to proceed. This is a key achievement!

Sexual recovery is not a calm ocean that you sail over like a stately ocean liner. You will still have your ups and downs. But in recovery, you have more access to hope. You know that you can change your sexual patterns, because you already have. The hopelessness of feeling out of control is no longer your constant state of being. As you gain hope, you also begin to gain personal power.

The Power to Change

For many people in recovery, the phrase *powerless over alcohol* will be deeply familiar. It is a foundational concept in AA, and millions have been helped by it. However, the feeling of powerlessness is also a painful feature of trauma. This means that "admitting" powerlessness may not feel clarifying; it may feel confusing or even demeaning.

When someone has exerted power over you in a way that causes you harm, you were not empowered to stop the harm in the moment.

If you have survived a trauma such as a car accident, natural disaster, incarceration, or military deployment to a combat zone, powerlessness is a nightmarish feature of the experience. This is also true for people who have survived the effects of structural injustices such as sexism, racism, homophobia, transphobia, ableism, and the myriad ways marginalization can cause us harm.

When the world you were born into was not built for you to thrive in it, powerlessness can be a feature of everyday life.

1. Where and when have you experienced the feeling of powerlessness? You can make a list, write a story, or note a day and time. Write down as much or as little as feels right for you today.

One important way we understand power is through financial freedom. A lack of economic power leads many women, nonbinary people, and gender-expansive people to stay in relationships that no longer fulfill them sexually or emotionally, or to stay with partners who are violent and abusive.

Our economic options mold and influence our sexual relationship decisions. We are not choosing partners in an ideal world of freedom and endless possibilities; we are engaging with real people while we all navigate prejudiced systems.

Given this reality, the more you know your own body, feelings, and desires, the more empowered you can be to advocate for the sexual life you want, regardless of your financial situation. You, caring for your body and developing an understanding of your own sexual feelings, are remaining as powerfully grounded in your own choices as is possible.

2. Have financial concerns affected your relationship or sexual choices? How? How do you feel about this now?

There may be times in our lives when making sexual choices is more an act of survival than of pleasure. The choice to trade sex for safety, drugs, a place to sleep, money, acceptance, the promise of a promotion, or anything else of value appears in many forms and at many different moments in our lives. It is not an uncommon experience for sex to become a commodity we can barter with.

Sexual recovery involves making these experiences conscious and understanding when you have felt empowered to choose how you engage sexually with others and when you haven't, or don't. Sometimes our choices change drastically when we become more aware of our power to choose. Sometimes we are engaged in the same behaviors, but how we feel about them changes.

Nova

When Nova first began working in a strip club, she was aware that she would be selling a sexual performance. She was comfortable showing her body and being in contact with men and women customers, and she did not feel ashamed of her work. Nova believed that consenting adults should have the right to private sexual transactions. When she started a recovery group for sex workers, Nova knew that it would feel much safer for her to talk about her work with people who had similar life experience. Although she did not primarily work as an escort or companion, she had spent many nights with customers—partying, getting high, having sex. She sometimes would receive cash gifts for her time and access to her body.

When Nova got sober, some of these sources of extra income dried up. She still did well dancing at her club, so she was able to stay financially stable, and slowly she built a clientele who were supportive of her sobriety.

Nova's online community was instrumental in supporting Nova through the challenges she faced. They met every week and helped each other maintain their commitments to their recovery. One issue many of them faced was the pressure they felt they were under to drink and do drugs with their clients. Some felt that it was easier just to say yes, even if it undermined their sobriety. Nova knew that wouldn't have worked for her.

"First, I really had to commit to not using alcohol and drugs of any kind," she told her peer group. "I wasn't a casual user; I was definitely addicted to meth, and alcohol often led to me using. So I just needed to back off completely.

"But also, I don't think being high made it easier to do sex work," Nova continued. "I think I would have said it did at the time, but really it made it harder. I had horrible hangovers all the time. I was embarrassed about stuff I'd said and done. I'd black out and not remember if I'd negotiated properly with a customer. Being high made me sloppy. It also kept me from knowing myself and what my real boundaries were."

"But isn't it harder to go in to work now?" a friend in the group asked.

Nova considered how to answer the question. "I'm more present in my body, and so I have to say no more often now, which is scary, because what if the customer gets mad or I don't get paid? But I still have clients because there are plenty of people who enjoy being with me as I am. I have clearer boundaries, which feels good to me. I go to bed feeling good about myself, and I wake up knowing what happened, and there's nothing I would trade for that peace of mind."

3. What would help you have more peace of mind in the present about your sexual choices?

Respecting Hopelessness

Hopelessness is a response to pain that seems intractable. It can creep in after years of recovery work, on a bad day, on the heels of a disappointment, a companion to a relapse, hiding in a hurtful conversation. It sounds like "I can't do this," "I don't want to do this anymore," "I should feel better by now," and "It never ends." When it all seems too, too hard, and the future is fearsome, hopelessness may take us over. This is a powerful experience and requires care and attention to move through.

Respecting hopelessness means recognizing and allowing the feeling to enter, and in doing so, feeling it fully, *without taking self-harming action*. In fact, the more gently and tenderly we can treat ourselves in the face of it, the more swiftly hopelessness will transform into something else. That something else only needs to be a sliver of light, a crack in the wall of pain.

4. If you have a memory of feeling hopeless, tell a story here. Even if you don't remember how you got out of that feeling, make sure that you acknowledge the change that occurred. You can use the model sentences below or create your own.

   I felt hopeless when:

   I started feeling better when:

If hopelessness visits you in your recovery process, ask someone you trust to sit alongside you as you let it roll through. If it persists and becomes an ongoing threat to your mental or physical health, you can call in more reinforcements: inpatient or outpatient programs, recovery groups, sponsors, accountability partners, professional therapists, loved ones, and so on.

It can help to have a safety plan already in place for yourself, so when you are in the middle of the difficulty, you already have resources ready.

5. Use the prompts below to create a safety plan:

   If I feel hopeless, I will call at least one of the following people:

   Self-soothing activities I can do that may help the feeling pass:

   Resources I trust (therapist, hotline, recovery group, etc.):

When we hit a wall of hopelessness, we are under a delusion that nothing will change. In fact, change comes whether we create it consciously or not. Time does not stop with our pain, and change is inevitable. Hopelessness is an indication that we are walking into our darker places and fearing that we may stay there.

Respecting hopelessness means allowing it but also moving through it. We feel, rest, and then try again tomorrow.

Suicide and Crisis Lifeline: Call or text 988

The Courage to Act

When you devote yourself to your own recovery from addiction and trauma, you may initially feel as if you are doing much of the work alone, but the truth is you are joining millions of other people who are trying to get better, just like you. When you commit to your sexual well-being, the same is true. Because sexuality is such a foundational part of who we are as humans (including those times when we are not sexually active or desirous), your curiosity and care for your sexual self can connect you to something much larger than you.

It takes immense courage, but you can take responsibility for where you are now and know that you are not alone.

6. For each of the statements below, recount an example from your life. If the statement isn't true for you, you can mark it and return to it later. You may notice opportunities arise to add examples once you are looking for them.

   I act in ways that reflect my values.

   Example:
   I remembered to call my friend on her birthday and tell her how much I care about her.

   I make amends where appropriate.

I respond consciously as new sexual situations happen.

I recognize where I may need or want more sexual education, and I seek out the information I need or want.

I exercise choice in how my sexual life unfolds.

I have the power to respond differently to familiar issues than I have in the past.

The path of growth, the upward spiral, is always a path that requires renewed choice on a daily basis. We grow in our ability to choose recovery and to choose a conscious path of self-empowerment. It is never easy or quick. Taking a step at a time, and allowing others to support those steps of growth, produces its own reward in a sense of well-being and a growing hope of the possibility of expansion.

Somatic Practice: Using Your Voice

This practice can be done sitting or lying down. You will want to be able to breathe as deeply and freely as possible. If you feel lightheaded at any point, return your breathing to normal until the feeling passes.

Place one hand on your chest, and on your next exhale, make a humming sound. See if you can feel the vibration against your hand, in your throat, or in your nose. For two more breaths, inhale deeply and exhale with a hum. You can vary the volume to your comfort and curiosity.

For the next three breaths, inhale through your nose and exhale through your mouth while making an *ahhh* sound that starts high and ends low. See if you can start higher and end lower each time. See if you can feel the vibration of the sound as it moves in your body.

For the next three breaths, inhale through your mouth and exhale through your mouth, making a loud sighing sound. You can add some more vibration to the sigh so it is like a groan. Sense how this sound relaxes and releases tension from your body.

For the last three breaths, inhale through your nose and exhale by making a humming sound again.

Place your hands in your lap or at your sides. Sit quietly for a minute or two as you allow your breath to return to normal. Notice any new sensations that arise as a result of this practice.

CHAPTER 9

Choosing Personal Power

Of what have I ever been afraid? To question or to speak as I believed could have meant pain, or death. But we all hurt in so many different ways, all the time, and the pain will either change or end. . . . And I began to recognize a source of power within myself that comes from the knowledge that, while it is most desirable not to be afraid, learning to put fear into a perspective gives me great strength. My silences had not protected me. Your silence will not protect you.

Audre Lorde, *Sister Outsider: Essays and Speeches*

Those of us in recovery keep ourselves from being able to use our personal power in many ways, but three are most common: by living in constant self-punishment for our destructive behavior in the past, by taking blame or inappropriate responsibility for abuse we endured, and by identifying with our shame more than our curiosity or pleasure.

When you choose to make changes in these areas, more empowerment, presence, and connection become possible. Sexuality can become creative, a source of energy and interest, rather than a place of fear, numbness, or indifference. This is where you feel empowered to choose and connect. It is where your personal power is cultivated and your pleasure is welcome. It takes time, but these changes are possible.

Guilt, Shame, and Self-Compassion

Guilt can have a positive function: It is a sign that we care about others' feelings, that we understand our own values, and that our behavior needs a course correction. We experience guilt when we feel that we have violated our own values, when we feel we have done something that goes against who we think we are or should be.

A pang of guilt about something we did in the past is a normal part of being a social human. It is a sign we want to take responsibility for our actions.

Once we have made our apologies, if they are possible and do not cause further harm, and take responsibility to adjust our behavior, guilt should begin to recede.

However, when we feel persistent, overwhelming guilt, we may struggle to live in the present, because we are stuck on something unresolved that we regret having done in the past.

1. Have you had a positive experience with making an apology to someone? Write out the memory here. If you don't have a memory of a positive experience of making an apology, imagine what that could look and feel like. What would make offering an apology a positive experience?

Guilt that persists, which becomes a heavier and heavier burden as time goes on, is an exhaustingly painful experience. For many people, this type of guilt morphs from "I am sorry for what I have done" into something more all-encompassing: "I am ashamed of who I am." If guilt is about what we have done, then shame is about who we believe we are. Shame can become a pervasive and constant feature of our emotional life.

2. Think of a time when you felt ashamed. What does shame feel like in your body? You can write or draw your experience here.

Shame enters through all levels of our experience, including our families, our communities, and our larger society. Shame is a consequence of personal events, such as being told there is something wrong with you by someone you trust. It is also a feature of systemic prejudice, which plays out in both large and small ways in every school, place of worship, workplace, community, city, county, and so on.

Shame is a cruel and slippery feature of surviving trauma, abuse, and addiction. We may know that we didn't want to be hurt, or to cause harm, but we still feel that we are no good at our very core. This feeling is so horrifying, so burdensome, that we become secretive about our shame. We don't want anyone to know how bad we are.

There is sometimes another twist: We feel we are supposed to be able to overcome shame simply and quickly. Therefore, when shame persists, we feel shame about our shame, as in, we become ashamed that we couldn't get better faster.

Taking a careful look at the source of shame in your life is an important step toward becoming more self-compassionate. You will certainly find that you have no control over many things. You may have internalized shame about any number of aspects of yourself, such as your gender, race, ethnicity, cultural background, where you grew up, what your body looks like, and your sexual preferences.

Some things about you can change, and others can't. Shame does not know the difference. It will show up to hurt you about parts of you that are completely unchangeable. But the variety we all embody is what gives life its rich complexity! If you are in touch with your wise inner observer self, you will know that there does not need to be shame attached to any of it. It is the prejudice of the world around you that is the problem.

3. I would like to release the shame I feel about:

As solid and impervious as shame may feel, you can eventually dissolve it. If pride in who you are feels far away because of how much guilt and shame you still carry, the work of self-compassion is the way to lighten your load. Self-compassion is an ongoing practice, a crucial part of recovery. Now, as we move along the upward spiral of recovery and healing, we will enrich our understanding of it.

One way that shame drains our power is by constantly berating us. Internally, you can begin to hear the voice of shame whenever you hear the word *should*.

There are definitely some *shoulds* in our life that are helpful and do not need to make us feel ashamed. For example: "If I want to pick up the kids on time, I should leave in five minutes." Or maybe "I'm feeling lonely today; I should look at my list of people I can call and try one of them." There's also "It was extremely stressful to me to set that boundary with my partner. I should pay attention to my body and support myself."

But that's not how most of us use *should*. We use it instead to tell ourselves we are wrong, broken, and lacking. Rather than allowing shame to bully you, you can gently reaffirm your inherent worth and dignity, identify resources that can support you in your feelings, and set the intention to care for yourself, no matter what. The following exercise is a chance to set this new intention in motion.

4. In the table below, you will make a list of shaming *should* statements on the left. You may have never spoken these statements aloud, but internally, they feel very real to you. Next, write a response to each from the perspective of your loving observer self. Remember, this is the part of you that loves you unconditionally, roots for you, and genuinely wants you to feel well, happy, connected to your sexuality, and safe.

Shaming statement	**Observer self response**
EXAMPLE: *It's been years since my trauma happened. I should be over it by now.*	*It's understandable that I get frustrated and impatient when I experience symptoms. Trauma healing can be unpredictable. Sometimes I will need extra support.*

Life After Sexual Trauma

Sexual violation can occur at a distance or up close, online or in person, and it can be confusing, especially if it happened with someone you were attracted to, while you were intoxicated, during something you originally consented to, or if it is difficult to remember clearly.

It can be tempting to compare your experience to others, to measure the intensity of your suffering after sexual trauma. Rather than try to decide "how bad" your experience was based on the imagined or real experiences of others, we encourage you to use your feelings in the present as your guide.

Whatever your lived experience, what matters is that you are honest with yourself about how you are doing, how you have been affected, and what support you need. This will open up space to imagine what is next for you and how you want to feel in your body, in your relationships, and in your sexuality.

Remember: No matter what you have experienced, you are not alone.

5. Read the following passage and write your responses below it.

> The statistics vary depending on the source, but somewhere between one in six and one in four women experience sexual assault (SA) in their lifetime.
>
> Until the latter half of the 1970s, it was not a crime in the United States for a man to force sexual intercourse on his wife. Marital rape was not recognized as a crime in all fifty states until 1993.
>
> Today's "rape shield laws" are designed to protect victims of SA from inquiry into their prior sexual conduct. They are in place because for most of the twentieth century, criminal courts allowed a man accused of rape to defend himself by pointing to a woman's reputation or prior sexual conduct.[1] In other words, "she asked for it" and "she deserved it" were viable legal defenses until very recently.
>
> Historians draw explicit connections from current sexual violence law back to our country's history of chattel slavery and colonial war against Indigenous peoples. Sexual violence against enslaved women was not only commonplace; it was not a crime in most states where slavery was legal. The restriction of tribal authority and imposition of colonial government ensured that there would be little to no accountability for violence against Native women.
>
> The positive changes that are happening now as a result of organized efforts are real, but they are also quite recent. Male entitlement to use violence against women's bodies has been repeated and reinforced for hundreds of years. It would be nearly impossible *not* to internalize the messages of rape culture as a source of shame.

What thoughts and feelings come up for you after reading this information?

Many who experience SA are also survivors of childhood sexual abuse (CSA). Sexual abuse during childhood isn't limited to the specific acts of fondling and penetration. It occurs across a continuum, from invasion of sexual privacy to unwanted comments about your body, being kissed in a way that felt uncomfortable, being touched when you didn't want to be, and being pressured to have sexual contact you didn't want. You may have been sexually mistreated in a variety of ways that you didn't initially identify as sexual abuse. Yet those instances can greatly affect your current sexual feelings and experiences.

Healing is possible. Women in recovery deal with the effects of SA and CSA in various ways. Many sexual trauma survivors find that both group process and individual therapy are helpful.

During ongoing recovery, you have the opportunity to look at past experiences that stand in the way of your own awakening and expansion. Although it takes a great deal of courage to face and tend to the pain without relying on the substances or behaviors that have numbed it, it is always worth the effort.

6. Today, I will give myself loving attention in the following ways:

Sexual trauma survivors may have been conditioned by negative sexual experiences to associate sex with helplessness, disgust, pain, anger, loss of control, shame, guilt, and even hate and rage. Therefore, it is often extremely difficult for survivors to experience sexuality with a deep sense of freedom. Sexual safety may not feel possible, or safety itself may not feel sexual.

The sexual challenges that result from sexual trauma do not go away by themselves. However, healing can occur, and survivors can make positive changes in the sexual areas of their lives. Survivors can move out of old, self-defeating patterns that reinforce unsatisfying sexual experiences and move into experiencing the kinds of sexual lives that they want. One activity to support this process is to identify a set of sexual rights and responsibilities.

7. Create two lists: your sexual rights and your sexual responsibilities.

My sexual rights	**My sexual responsibilities**
EXAMPLES: *The right to say yes* *The right to say no* *The right to feel safe* *The right to experiment*	*Making sure I am listening to my partner when they say yes and no* *Listening to my own body* *Not pushing myself past what feels good to me*

Go through your list of sexual rights and note each one that is not now an integral part of your sexual life. Ask yourself why you don't feel you have that right. Explore why you might be afraid to have that right or what other form of resistance you may have. Visualize yourself having that right and see what you would have to do to create it for yourself.

Note your reflections here:

Do the same for the responsibilities. Note your reflections here:

Michelle and Chris

When Michelle created her list of rights and responsibilities, she was overwhelmed with guilt and fear. She realized how many times she had had sex with her husband, Chris, when she didn't want to, out of a sense of obligation or to avoid a conflict when she was drunk, and it was difficult for her to face. She thought of herself as the more sexual partner in their marriage, but during her sobriety, she realized she had often thought of sex as a way to keep Chris happy and off her back about her drinking. As a couple, they had not been focusing on her pleasure, and she wanted to talk with Chris about this without hurting his pride.

Because Michelle had been practicing self-compassion, she was able to remind herself that what she had done in the past was what she thought best in the moment, and now she was equipped to make new choices. She was still afraid that if she told her husband she wanted to do things differently, he would resist. He had been getting more of what he wanted, overall, she thought, and she was concerned that he would be angry with her once they started talking about her right to say no.

She was surprised, then, when she brought up this issue in couple's therapy and he seemed relieved that they were finally going to talk about it. The therapist gently guided the conversation, and Michelle was able to express some dissatisfaction with their sexual habits. Even with many months of sobriety from alcohol, Michelle had felt this issue was too difficult to broach. Chris nodded along as she described their struggle to reconnect sexually after such a long time of avoiding each other.

"Sometimes I'm so relieved that he wants to have sex with me that I'll just go with it, even if I'm not physically turned on," Michelle said, and she felt the tears begin to rise. "I feel guilty. I feel stupid. I want better for me, for him, for us both. We used to just fall into bed with so much passion for each other."

Chris chimed in. "I never want to make you do something you don't really want to do. When I think about your assault, I feel disgusted by the man who hurt you, and I never, ever want to do anything that would hurt you." They were able to meet each other's gaze. This was something Michelle didn't know she needed to hear, but it was a huge relief and reassurance that her husband was thinking about her boundaries this way.

With time and care, Michelle and Chris started unpacking how fearful they both had been about their sexual connection. They both had experienced a sense of rejection, a fear of approaching their partner with desire, and a feeling of being stuck in old habits. Once they were able to speak these honest feelings out loud, they could begin to create new ways to communicate, support each other, and explore new ways to connect sexually.

Beyond Self-Punishment

Most people who experience CSA and SA will not see their abusers/attackers take any responsibility or endure real consequences. The very few who use the criminal legal system may face a series of painful, retraumatizing events as they come to recognize the harm that was caused. This lack of community accountability leaves many of us feeling unsettled, and often, we turn our pain back inward. In the absence of justice, we are more likely to punish ourselves.

Self-punishment does not help us come to terms with abuse we experienced. It also does not "fix" our own harmful behavior in the past. We must move away from constant self-punishment, even if we have not yet been forgiven for everything we were responsible for, even if we wish we could tell a story about the past in which we were in control at all times, knowing deep down that we simply weren't. No one is in control of everything that happens all the time.

The way we characterize our own behavior matters for our ongoing recovery. Taking responsibility for ourselves is different from relentless self-punishment.

8. What does it feel like to punish myself?

   What does it feel like to take accountability for what I am responsible for?

What does self-compassion mean to me?

Ongoing recovery is a time of deeper changes. As the layers of guilt and shame begin to peel away, and you develop more self-compassion, you can connect more with your current desires. Your capacity to know how you feel is directly related to your ability to consciously experience your body's sensations. When you are engaged with your body's sensations, you are listening to how your body responds to both your external and internal environments. Tuning in to your sensations without judgment is part of cultivating compassion for yourself.

You can create a sense of personal sexual dignity, empowering yourself to act on your sexuality without violating or coercing others, and becoming accountable for your sexual self and your recovery. Working with the issues that have kept you from empowerment and responsibility, such as shame, will enable you to experience intimacy with yourself and with those you love. As you grow in self-compassion, your capacity for pleasure will also grow.

Somatic Practice: Stomping Ground

Stand with enough room around you to swing your arms. If you need to modify the practice to remain seated, you may want a tabletop surface within reach.

For about a minute, swing your arms and stomp your feet in an exaggerated marching movement. Every time your right foot hits the ground, your left arm swings forward, and you say or think the word *here*. Every time your left foot hits the ground, your right arm swings forward, and you say or think the word *now*. For those who need to remain seated, a light strike to the tabletop can serve as a stomp.

Raise your knees and let your stomps resonate throughout your whole body. You may be thinking a lot about your past, but you are present here and now. Let your body be grounded in the present moment.

After about a minute of this practice, stand or sit quietly with your eyes closed or lowered. Notice how your body feels and what thoughts are coming to your mind. When you have spent a minute in quiet, you can open your eyes.

PART

4

Awakening to Intimacy

Experiencing authentic intimacy is one of the most hope-filled and exhilarating aspects of being human. As we progress in our healing, we are more able to experience the kind of trust between individuals that produces equality, mutuality, and reciprocity. Intimacy is a form of connection that deepens and enriches our lives. It is something we can feel with ourselves and in relationships with others. Developing these dynamics between yourself and others is a lifelong task.

Awakening to intimacy and awakening to your sexuality are interrelated. Both are dimensions of the ongoing process of recovery. In recovery we begin to understand what we have longed for, what we really want in our lives. This next level of awakening poses an exciting challenge for all of us, no matter where we are on this path.

CHAPTER 10

Developing Self-Intimacy

Be willing to look in every corner and under all the rugs and closets to find the lost parts of you that were stashed and swept into the cracks and crannies. They are waiting for the thick medicinal salve of your patient, loving attention. Stay with your heart in all weather. Stay warm.

Pixie Lighthorse, *The Wound Makes the Medicine: Elemental Remediations for Transforming Heartache*

What is intimacy? A simple way to think of it is deep, honest, safe, trusting connection that brings a sense of joy and satisfaction to our lives. As we move toward establishing real intimacy in our relationships, it becomes clear that intimacy with ourselves is our foundation for intimacy with others.

Both sexuality and intimacy are complex human experiences. There are different ways of experiencing and expressing intimacy. Emotional intimacy involves sharing our feelings; intellectual intimacy involves sharing our thoughts; physical intimacy involves sharing our bodies, not always in sexual ways.

We live in a society that confuses and mixes together love, sex, and intimacy. Often when we're looking for one, we go out and get another. When you're looking for intimacy, you may end up in a sexual encounter, but the fact that it is sexual does not make it intimate. Conversely, you may be very intimate with someone with whom you are not sexual at all.

Love is also a huge word, encompassing multiple forms of relationship: familial, romantic, friendship, and so on. We can feel love for someone without experiencing intimacy with them. Partnerships can be fluid, too, sometimes filled with sexual connection and other times not, while the love and intimacy remain. One partner may feel just as intimate without sexual connection, while the other requires sex to feel close.

This is why knowing yourself, being in tune with your own feelings, needs, and desires, and developing an intimate relationship with yourself is such an important part of recovery.

Addiction interferes with the ability to experience deep connection with others; our perceptions become distorted, our behavior becomes defensive, our feelings become altered. In recovery we learn to recognize these processes in their early stages and change our direction. To know ourselves this deeply means taking responsibility for not only our behavior, but the thinking and feeling that leads us to it.

Being intimate with yourself does not mean being narcissistic, obsessing endlessly about yourself and your own wants and needs. It does not mean you have to focus on yourself to the exclusion of others. It means knowing who you are, being in touch with your feelings as they occur, and feeling curious about why you react to events and situations as you do. It means committing to your own sexual life, regardless of whether you are sharing physical connection with another person. It can mean sex with yourself, exploring your fantasies, and learning about what makes you excited. Self-intimacy is the practice of being your own best friend, partner, lover, and wise guide.

Knowing yourself includes knowing your feelings, body, mind, spirit, and sexuality. Ultimately, these are not discrete layers of you—they are all connected, overlapping, and intertwined. As you move up the spiral of recovery and healing, you will discover more about who you are now, and who you are becoming.

Know Your Feelings

Feelings are inevitable. They are a valuable source of information about who we are and what we are experiencing. You do not have to judge them, deny them, or act upon them; it is enough to feel and observe them. You can decide how to take action after first spending time with your feelings. Some common feelings after addiction and trauma are anger, hurt, fear, anxiety, shame, and numbness.

Many people try to stop feeling altogether, thinking it is safer. Feelings do not operate like a faucet—we can't turn on the warm side and leave the cold side off. When we are ready to thaw out and feel our feelings, we are going to feel both the pleasant and the unpleasant. With time, practice, and care, even uncomfortable feelings become an opportunity for self-knowledge and self-intimacy. As we gain self-supportive skills and tolerance for our intense feelings, we become more able to connect with our own lives and other people.

Many recovering people have a lifetime of stored-up, unexpressed feelings buried underneath today's mood. It is common to repress big feelings like grief or rage, because we fear being overwhelmed and engulfed by their intensity and strength. Luckily, the skills of identifying, experiencing, and choosing how to express feelings can be developed at any time.

1. Knowing your feelings takes practice. When you tune in to your feelings in this moment, what do you notice? Remember, feelings do not always match the situation in front of you. They are often connected to the past and future, and many people experience more than one at once.

   Circle any of the words on the following list that apply to you right now, and add more to the list as you identify them.

   Right now I am feeling:

angry	hurt	fearful	anxious
numb	depressed	relaxed	interested
calm	powerful	joyful	connected
lonely	irritated	sad	disappointed
frustrated	afraid	remorseful	playful
jealous	surprised	stressed	courageous
tender			

How challenging is it for you to identify your feelings? Why do you think this is so?

Know Your Body

Your body is a treasury of knowledge about yourself. How and what your body feels can tell you a great deal about what's going on with you. Often, feelings you don't express emotionally find expression through your body. Headaches, stomachaches, backaches, muscle tension, hypertension, and breathing disorders may all be signals that a strong feeling needs your attention.

Because we most often express our sexuality with our body, knowing our body precedes a full knowledge of who we are as an expressive sexual being.

One way to think about feelings is that they must be metabolized, like food. What is nutritive will be used, and what is not nourishing needs to be passed through the body. We exhale, cry, laugh, shake, sleep, sweat, and excrete—feelings can affect and be affected by all these processes.

Rather than pushing through pain and ignoring the signs that our body is offering us, sexual recovery asks us to slow down, listen, and give our body what it needs. While breath, food, water, and shelter are first-order human needs to stay alive, we have other needs that also must be met for us to thrive. These include movement, connective touch, and time spent in natural space.

Movement

Patterned, rhythmic, repetitive movement is key to processing emotions. The movement that works for you will be unique to your body. One of the most accessible to most people is walking. Even a short ten-minute walk can help bring you back to yourself.

You can also bounce a ball against a wall, sway your body side to side, or pat your body gently from head to toe. If you enjoy more intense physical sensations, you can lift weights, try a martial art, or attend a group fitness class. Engaging in a movement practice is not about getting exercise, although that can be a benefit. It is about movement, period. Moving the body encourages movement of feelings.

2. Try ten minutes of gentle movement of your choice, and note your reflections here.

   Date: ____________ Time: ____________ Movement type: ___________________________

   How I feel after this practice:

Connective Touch

Recent research suggests that a lack of regular, daily connective touch has significant negative emotional and psychological impacts. If you do not have people near you who feel safe to hug, cuddle with, hold, or even sit next to, it is time to seek them out.

If it is financially possible, seeking massage, acupressure, or other bodywork techniques may also help. There are communities in most cities dedicated to safe cuddling, where you can attend gatherings where people practice consent, maintain boundaries, and offer each other supportive touch. Sometimes we think we need or want sex when it is connective touch we are seeking.

3. Notice the presence or absence of connective touch in your life.

   Are you in need of more connective, supportive touch from other people?

   Do you know how to offer it to yourself?

   What type of touch would feel replenishing and nourishing to you right now?

Time in Nature

Your body is not separate from the natural world; it is part of it. Some people have consistent contact with the natural space around them—they live or work in places where plants, animals, soil, sky, and seasons are part of everyday life. Increasingly, more humans live in cities, where regular contact with nature is more difficult to come by. In most cities, there is some green space afforded to the public in the way of parks, trails, walkways, or playgrounds. You don't need a large expanse of mind-blowing mountains; you just need to regularly prioritize putting your body closer to the natural world.

4. Find five minutes to connect with the natural world. You can stop and watch an ant as it makes its way across a bench. You can slip your shoes off and put your feet in the grass. You can sniff the scent of the earth after a rain. You can look up into the sky at night and notice the moon. Below, make a note of what you did to connect with the natural world.

   Date: ________ Time: ________

   What I did to connect with the natural world:

How I felt after this practice:

Know Your Mind

Becoming familiar with your thinking can be very exciting, and it can also bring awareness of difficult inner dialogue. As you tune in to your body, you will likely also be hearing from your mind. Ongoing recovery invites you to investigate how your mind works, what triggers a thought process, how you solve problems, what prevents you from thinking clearly about an issue, and more.

Understanding your mind's abilities and awareness of how your mind works are part of your path to greater self-intimacy.

Remember that self-compassion needs to lead the way. You get to decide which of your thoughts best indicate who you are, and you do not need to overidentify with self-harming or unwanted thoughts. They are clues about your pain, and they do need your attention to be resolved, but they are not all of who you are.

If you find that your mind is constantly criticizing you or others, flashing ahead to scary future possibilities, or stuck replaying painful past events, you may need to recruit more support. Anxiety, depression, and symptoms like intrusive thoughts can overwhelm the mind. If the thoughts feel too powerful and lead to overwhelming feelings, it is time to ask for help.

As you reclaim your thinking, you will also begin to clarify your thoughts on sex. You may begin to see how your sexual thinking affects your choices. Perhaps you make assumptions about how other people feel, or you have judgments about your own or others' desires. Perhaps you get frustrated during sexual situations because your mind doesn't seem to "turn off."

Our minds can also provide the antidote. We can call upon our loving observer self to remind us that our bodies are worthy of love and pleasure, and we are safe in the present moment. It is good to feel all of our feelings, and it is good to breathe through them as they change.

5. Remember a time when you were experiencing pleasure, sexual or otherwise. Can you recall what was going on in your mind? Try to describe the experience here.

Your efforts to become more aware of your body and mind are directly linked to your capacity to enjoy sexual feelings. Sexual feelings ask us to stay in the present moment. Staying in the present takes practice and attention, but it is rewarding. The more you try to do it, the more you will be able to do it.

Know Your Spirit

A fundamental part of knowing yourself is knowing your spiritual self, investigating that part of who you are that connects you to something larger. Whether you think of this mysterious aspect as God or Goddess, Higher Power, consciousness, electrical impulses in the brain, a reincarnated soul, the connectedness of life on Earth, or something else—that is something you decide for yourself. We use the term *spirit* here because it captures an idea, but of course that idea may not fit in with your beliefs. If *spirit* doesn't sound right for you, please feel free to imagine simply the facts: Each of us is always part of something larger than ourselves, and we are alive now because of the generations of people who lived before us.

It can be difficult to respect your spiritual needs in a society that appears so focused on the material, external, and urgent. Knowing yourself spiritually is not simply knowing what you believe; it also includes recognizing and validating your longings by taking time out of your busy life to fulfill those needs. As you search for wholeness, harmony, and connection to yourself, other people, and the world, you will come to know who you are. You will develop a deeper understanding of what it means to you to be alive in this body for the time that you have.

The feeling of ecstasy, which we tend to connect with physical pleasure, was considered by many ancients to be a merging with the divine, truly heaven on earth. In ongoing recovery, you will learn to honor the sexual part of yourself as an irreplaceable and integral aspect of the sacredness of your being.

6. How do you honor your spiritual self or meet your need for a sense of interconnectedness?

Know Your Sexuality

For some people, sexual identity is clear and fixed—they have certainty about whom they are attracted to and what they do and do not enjoy, and they can name the reasons why they might want to have sex. For many others, sexual identity is not quite so predictable and defined. If you are still learning about your sexual self, take heart.

Knowing your sexuality does not mean defining yourself with a label and never revising it. Knowing your sexuality means giving awareness and attention to your feelings, allowing yourself to have fantasies and desires that surprise you, and listening to what your body tells you.

Although our society socializes us to be exclusively heterosexual for our whole lives, the reality of human sexual identity is a complex and varied spectrum. You are free to explore your sexual identity without having to categorize yourself into a rigid definition that may not fit your experience or feelings. At the same time, for some people having labels feels important and safe—it validates their experience and helps them feel connected to a community.

No one really knows how any particular sexual identity develops. The only facts we're clear about are that all sexual identities are valid, that they can be complex, and that they can change and develop over time. Whether you feel sure or uncertain, new to this conversation or experienced, spending some time asking yourself the following questions is a valuable exercise in knowing your sexuality more deeply.

7. Answer the following questions three times: first for who you are today, again for who you were before a recovery process; and last for your ideal future self—where you'd like to be. These three sets of answers will give you some idea of how your sexual identity has developed and what direction you'd like to move in.

PRESENT SELF

Fantasies:

Whom and what are your fantasies about?

Do you fantasize about particular acts with particular people?

If you do not currently fantasize, did you do so in the past? Can you remember when or why you stopped?

If you never have fantasized, what does it feel like to try?

Are there any books, movies, shows, music, or other media that fuel your fantasies?

Eroticism:

What feels erotic—sensual, sexy, exciting—to you?

Are there particular bodies you find more erotic than others? Do you find particular physical characteristics erotic?

Can you feel erotic with yourself alone?

Do you feel erotic when out in nature, dancing, eating a rich meal, or something else?

Do you feel excited by feelings of danger, humiliation, degradation, dominance, or control?

Are there particular smells, tastes, textures, or sounds that are erotic for you?

Emotional attachments:

Where do your strongest emotional attachments lie?

Are you equally attached to people of different genders, or do you find your strongest attachments tend to be with a certain gender?

Whom are your emotional bonds and connections with?

With whom do you wish to connect?

Sexual behavior:

What is your sexual experience?

With whom have you had sexual activity?

Does your sexual experience align with what you find erotic?

Are there sexual experiences you want to have for the first time or repeat from the past?

What are your habits and patterns around masturbation?

Now answer the questions again. This time try to recreate your experiences prior to entering a recovery or healing process. Imagine how your past self would respond to these questions.

PAST SELF

Fantasies:

Whom and what are your fantasies about?

Do you fantasize about particular acts with particular people?

If you do not currently fantasize, did you do so in the past? Can you remember when or why you stopped?

If you never have fantasized, what does it feel like to try?

Are there any books, movies, shows, music, or other media that fuel your fantasies?

Eroticism:

What feels erotic to you?

Are there particular bodies you find more erotic than others? Do you find particular physical characteristics erotic?

Can you feel erotic with yourself alone?

Do you feel erotic when out in nature, dancing, eating a rich meal, or something else?

Do you feel excited by feelings of danger, humiliation, degradation, dominance, or control?

Are there particular smells, tastes, textures, or sounds that are erotic for you?

Emotional attachments:

Where do your strongest emotional attachments lie?

Are you equally attached to people of different genders, or do you find your strongest attachments tend to be with a certain gender?

Whom are your emotional bonds and connections with?

With whom do you wish to connect?

Sexual behavior:

What is your sexual experience?

With whom have you had sexual activity?

Does your sexual experience align with what you find erotic?

Are there sexual experiences you want to have for the first time or repeat from the past?

What are your habits and patterns around masturbation?

Finally, answer the following questions again with an eye toward the future. Imagine yourself in two to three years. Importantly, this version of you is feeling well and enjoying your sexual self. What would this version of you like to explore? What does this version of you find satisfying or interesting sexually?

FUTURE SELF

Fantasies:

Whom and what are your fantasies about?

Do you fantasize about particular acts with particular people?

If you do not currently fantasize, did you do so in the past? Can you remember when or why you stopped?

If you never have fantasized, what does it feel like to try?

Are there any books, movies, shows, music, or other media that fuel your fantasies?

Eroticism:

What feels erotic to you?

Are there particular bodies you find more erotic than others? Do you find particular physical characteristics erotic?

Can you feel erotic with yourself alone?

Do you feel erotic when out in nature, dancing, eating a rich meal, or something else?

Do you feel excited by feelings of danger, humiliation, degradation, dominance, or control?

Are there particular smells, tastes, textures, or sounds that are erotic for you?

Emotional attachments:

Where do your strongest emotional attachments lie?

Are you equally attached to people of different genders, or do you find your strongest attachments tend to be with a certain gender?

Whom are your emotional bonds and connections with?

With whom do you wish to connect?

Sexual behavior:

What is your sexual experience?

With whom have you had sexual activity?

Does your sexual experience align with what you find erotic?

Are there sexual experiences you want to have for the first time or repeat from the past?

What are your habits and patterns around masturbation?

Read back through your answers to this exercise and reflect on what you see. Below, make note of any meaningful similarities and differences among your current, past, and imagined future selves.

Example:

My past self had no fantasy life—there didn't seem to be anything to look forward to. My current and future selves are full of ideas for experiences I'd like to have.

It can be difficult to face the impacts of sexual trauma on our capacity for pleasure, desire, intimacy, and connection. There may have been a time in the past when you felt more curious, free, and safe with sex. Or there may have been very little time in which you felt "innocent," especially if you experienced CSA. Answering these questions can reveal places where your sexual self has been stuck, hiding, or afraid. Remember that self-knowledge does not need to be put into practice immediately. You can stay gentle with yourself and make changes that feel safe.

Knowing your sexuality and knowing what your body looks and feels like during sexual arousal go hand in hand. In chapter 4, you took a look at your genitals in the mirror. Now, you can explore your body's sexual responses with even more gentle curiosity.

8. Begin by setting yourself up well: Get as physically comfortable as you can, in a time and place when you are able to have privacy. Set up a mirror so you can watch how your genitals change with arousal. We highly recommend using a lubricant—any type that works for your body. If you have physical limitations that prevent you from reaching your genitals with your hands, please feel free to use any assistive devices you may already have. If you are used to masturbating with a vibrator, feel free to have it handy.

You may want to take a few minutes to touch more of your body before you begin touching your genitals. Explore your belly, hips, butt, and thighs with your hands, preparing your body for more pleasure.

When you are ready to touch your genitals, begin with soft, gentle strokes, moving slowly. Notice if your skin color changes with arousal; notice any changes with increased blood flow to your genitals. You may notice an increase in lubrication. Many women will be able to see when their clitoris enlarges and becomes erect, then later retracts and becomes hidden. For others, the visible change is not as pronounced, but the sensations usually change as the clitoris fills with blood. Enjoy the sensations and relax into your curiosity about your own body.

While this exercise does not emphasize orgasm, you are free to enjoy your body any way you choose. When you feel finished with the activity of exploring your body's responses, please take your time to reset and then return to the workbook to complete the exercise.

When you are ready, reflect on this exercise. What did you notice? How did it make you feel to watch your body's responses?

Trauma, compulsive behaviors, substance dependence, and the stress of beginning recovery all affect how our bodies respond to stimuli, even our familiar ways of masturbating. For example, one woman who did this exercise realized that she had been masturbating with a very strong vibrator for years, thinking that she had difficulty orgasming because her clitoris was "not that sensitive." It turned out that when she gave herself time to slowly become more aroused and touched more of her own body with her hands, she wanted much less direct clitoral stimulation than she expected. She had developed her masturbation habits while using cocaine, and years later, her body had different needs. When she slowed down and allowed her body time to warm up, she had powerful orgasms with a less intense vibrator.

Knowing how to reliably bring yourself to orgasm means you can take responsibility for your own pleasure. When your partners no longer have to guess at what you're in the mood for and are relieved of the full responsibility of satisfying you sexually, they too are freed up to be more experimental and more responsive. When you know what excites you and what brings you to orgasm, you can begin to communicate this clearly to your partners.

Self-intimacy is rooted in self-knowledge. Knowing your own body, mind, spirit, and sexuality, especially when you can view what you find through the lens of self-compassion, creates space for sexual flourishing. You may choose to continue this journey on your own, or from inside a preexisting partnership. You will be entering a new phase of your life in which you build your relationships on a stronger foundation. The next chapter will focus on how you can bring your new skills into relationships with other people.

Somatic Practice: Go with the Flow

Begin this practice in a comfortable standing position. If standing is difficult, feel free to do the practice while seated, and modify it in the ways that work for you.

Gently lower or close your eyes. Take a few slow and steady breaths, and begin to visualize that you are in a warm ocean environment. Your feet are rooted into the sand, and you are a tall aquatic plant. Allow your body to begin to move with the waves and tides. Keep your feet in one place, but allow any and all of the rest of you to bend, swirl, wave, and swish with the water. Move your body in ways that feel gentle and releasing. You may enjoy raising your hands and arms above your head and feeling a gentle wave roll along your whole body. Experience how it feels to go with the flow around you. Do this practice for two to three minutes, breathing gently and fully throughout.

When you have returned to stillness, take a few moments to notice the feelings and sensations that may have arisen in the practice.

CHAPTER 11

Creating Deeper Connections with Others

If we were constantly remembering that love is as love does, we would not use the word in a manner that devalues and degrades its meaning. When we are loving, we openly and honestly express care, affection, responsibility, respect, commitment, and trust.

bell hooks, *All About Love: New Visions*

Great sex can happen in a wide variety of circumstances—with or without intimacy, with someone you barely know or know extremely well, spontaneously or after careful planning. However, a great *sexual relationship* is nourishing, sustaining, pleasurable, and growth-fostering. It takes skill to maintain. The first skill is friendship.

For those who are currently partnered, this chapter will offer tools for creating greater intimacy in current relationships. For those seeking new romantic and sexual relationships, this chapter will lay the groundwork for creating honest connections that can flourish over time, with care. For those who are not seeking sexual partnership at this time, this chapter will affirm the importance of cultivating intimacy in friendships.

Nourishing Friendships

Have you ever noticed a friend of yours who seems to disappear each time she is dating someone new? Or perhaps you are that person, who finds it difficult to maintain your friendships when there is a new partner in your life. Many people find themselves concentrating on their sexual relationships to the detriment of their friendships.

Taking the time to nurture and maintain our friendships is not easy, but it is essential to our sustenance and nourishment. Having a friend who has known you and supported you over time, no matter how frequently or infrequently you see one another, helps to remind you of the reality of your experiences, the continuity of your life, and your value and presence in someone else's life. Maintaining friendships is also part of maintaining your independent self and can help prevent you from getting lost in someone new.

While some friendships may include sexual attraction and even be sexual relationships, this discussion is about friendships that do not include sexuality as a feature. At the same time, it is important to note that the qualities we develop and deepen in friendship are the same ones that can make our long-term sexual relationships meaningful: honesty, vulnerability, support, playfulness, curiosity, commitment, mutuality, and shared power.

1. Consider the friendships in your life. For each of the statements below, write the name or names of the friend(s) that the statement describes best. If no one comes to mind, you can consider whether this is a quality you'd like to deepen in your friendships.

______________	We experience a reciprocal interest in giving and receiving attention.
______________	We have a mutual desire to create and maintain the relationship.
______________	We both find the friendship important and value it in a similar manner.
______________	We express similar degrees of vulnerability and ability to trust.
______________	We both put energy into being together.
______________	We listen to and support one another.
______________	We help each other understand when something we have said or done has had a negative impact.
______________	We apologize to each other when necessary, and we receive the other's apology with an open heart.
______________	I feel seen, heard, and known when we are together.
______________	We influence each other in positive ways.

_______________ I feel safe to share my inner thoughts, feelings, desires, and needs with them.

_______________ We honestly communicate and navigate conflict with care.

_______________ We support each other through life's changes.

What thoughts and feelings arose about your friendships while you read through the statements above?

Dating New People

Talking about sexuality in early dating relationships can feel overwhelming, so much so that many people simply do not do it. If you are dating while sober, you may find that you used to rely on alcohol or other substances to bridge the gap between a flirtation and a sexual experience. Now you have to do it yourself, and it can be difficult to know where to start.

Those who use dating apps are navigating a sometimes bewildering set of questions when they start talking to someone new. While dating apps have made it more common for people to openly discuss their likes/dislikes and relationship goals, they have not yet cured our culture of embarrassment, shame, and inequality when it comes to sexuality.

In the early stages of dating someone new, you and your partner will set up habits around your sexual connection, and you can take responsibility for creating habits that foster pleasure and open communication. Your partner is a full participant in creating those habits.

2. The following questions, while centering the experience of dating a new person, can also shed light on how you currently feel about having conversations about sexual topics with your current partner:

   How comfortable do you feel talking with a new person (or current partner) about your sexual health?

   Do you know what you prefer when using barriers for STIs? If pregnancy prevention is important, what is the plan?

   How does your partner respond when you ask for a particular type of touch or sexual activity?

   How curious does your partner seem about your body and your pleasure?

   How able are you to respond with kindness and open curiosity to your partner's requests for a particular type of touch or sexual activity?

   How able to say "no" do you feel?

3. It's time to practice your communication skills! Here are practical steps for discussing sexual health practices and sexual preferences with someone new. With an established partner, you can choose any sexuality topic you'd like to discuss. Follow the steps below, and make note of how the conversation went.

    a. Start the conversation before you are kissing, touching, or in bed.

    b. Sit with some space between you, such as at a table.

    c. Allow your partner to choose to opt in to the conversation now or to have it at another time. Some helpful conversation starters might be:

        "I'd like to check in about our sexual health; is now a good time?"

        "I like to talk about sex before it's happening; is that okay with you?"

        "I'm excited for where this is going! Can we check in about a few things, like our safer sex practices and sexual preferences?"

    d. Begin with the basics: Share your STI and testing status. Share your safer sex practice preferences, and if pregnancy prevention is an issue, discuss it. Share if you have other partners and whether you are using safer sex methods with them so your new partner is aware of their level of risk and can make informed decisions. (For established partners, you can check in about the methods you are currently using and make sure you agree they are the best for your current needs.)

        If you know that you have strong sexual preferences—for example, you enjoy practicing BDSM and want a partner who can participate—share a bit about yourself. Then ask your partner if there is anything else they want to know. Ask them to share a bit with you about the same topics. (For established partners, now is a time to talk about new sexual activities you'd like to try and gauge their interest.)

    e. Be kind to yourself no matter how it goes. Remember that sex cannot be ruined by open communication. At any point, it is okay to table the conversation for another time. You do not need to tell all your stories of sexual trauma to a new person. What you *do* need is to gauge their comfort with conversations about sexual topics and their capacity to listen for and respect boundaries.

Make notes on your experience using the above steps. How did the conversation go? How do you feel after having open dialogue with your partner about a sexuality topic?

Keep the door open. The goal here is sexual pleasure without fear. Perhaps you will need to negotiate boundaries around certain sexual activities or talk about what kind of sexual communication you both prefer. Ongoing communication is always preferable.

Falling in Love

You may be propelled into becoming more emotionally and sexually connected to another by the experience of falling in love. The feeling of falling for someone can be very vulnerable. You may idealize your potential partner, seeing in them someone who can meet all your needs, who has the qualities you want, and who will be able to love you as you have always wanted to be loved.

Once you become more connected to another person sexually and emotionally, you begin to know who that person really is. Usually at that point, the idealized image begins to fade away, and the real person becomes clearer to you.

Now comes a more mature choice. Ask yourself, “Is this someone I want to maintain a connection with? Is this someone I want to build a relationship with?” If you can honestly answer yes, then you can begin taking some calculated emotional risks. This is how you build the kind of intimate love relationship that will sustain and nurture you, by deepening your relationship in evolutionary stages.

4. How do you currently feel about your life experience of falling in love?

Arati

After dating a new person for a few months, Arati would usually find that she could not live without the euphoric feelings she had in the idealization stage of falling in love. She would find herself beginning to back away from the relationship when the idealization started to fade. She would tell herself it "wasn't meant to be" because her feelings had started to change.

Instead of choosing to build an intimate sexual relationship, she would go looking for someone else to fall in love with, and she would abandon the next relationship, too, as the initial euphoria faded into the attentiveness and decision-making required by authentic connection.

For years, Arati dated new people, going from relationship to relationship, seeking those magical moments, in an addictive search for the high of being in love. Deeper intimacy never had time to develop. She used to tell herself that she would just know when it was right, and that she owed it to herself and her son not to settle for someone who didn't keep her happy.

Arati's most recent partner had ended their dating relationship before Arati ran away, which was a rare experience for her. She realized that she had not been able to show up fully to the relationship because of her out-of-control behaviors with alcohol and prescription pills. She regretted not putting more care into the relationship, and she saw it as a chance for deeper intimacy that had been lost.

For a while, she tried to convince her ex-partner to try again. They told her they didn't see what would be different between them, and gently but firmly said no. Arati was hurt and angry, and she argued that her sobriety changed everything.

Later, in therapy, Arati was able to accept that her ex-partner had made a decision, and that the most loving thing she could do was respect the boundary, allow herself to grieve, and take good care of herself. Importantly, she realized that her sobriety hadn't changed everything after all. Her desire for the high of a new relationship was threaded throughout her life. Her difficulty trusting someone and allowing a relationship to grow was still present for her.

Now that she is focusing on her sobriety and self-pleasure, Arati feels more equipped to try dating again. She still has concerns about what it will look and feel like to build deeper intimacy with someone new. It scares her to imagine being consistently open, honest, vulnerable, and committed to someone, but it is a fear she'd like to face.

Learning to be comfortable in a new sexual relationship may take time. It will certainly require that you take emotional risks, and inevitably there will be bumps in the road.

You may find yourself feeling stuck in a relationship with a sexual partner who can't match you in a respectful, mutual, compassionate relationship. You may put your trust in people who eventually disappoint you. These situations will not be as devastating if you have developed a strong, grounded sense of intimacy with yourself and supportive friends.

5. Your answers to the following questions will help you determine whether your sexual relationships have the capacity for intimacy.

   Do we have a sense of mutual respect?

Do we have a mutual understanding about the level of emotional depth we want in our relationship? Do we agree on how much or how little emotional involvement we would like to have with each other?

What happens when we have conflict? Do we work it out safely and with compassion?

Do we assume good intentions from each other?

Do I feel seen and understood? Does my partner indicate to me that they feel seen and understood?

Do we support each other's growth?

Are we honest with each other?

Do we help each other reach our goals?

Do I feel safe to be my full self with them?

Note that if you are nonmonogamous, you may have different answers to these questions for different partners. Perhaps you have identified a partner with whom you are not seeking deeper intimacy, but having a sexual and/or romantic connection with them is still enjoyable and fulfilling in your life. There are no rules that say every person has to achieve the highest level of intimacy possible to be a positive force in your life.

Maybe you don't have answers to some of these questions yet, or maybe you found you had to answer no to a few of them when you wish you could have said yes. Only you can decide what is the next best step given what you have identified. Perhaps you can talk to your partner about an area of your relationship where you would like to grow and change together. Working with a couple's therapist can help facilitate the process of creating intimacy when difficulties are present. Falling in love brings us together, but conscious decisions bring us sustained intimacy.

If you decide that your current sexual partner is someone with whom you'd like to become more intimate, you'll need to realize that doing so is a process that takes time. Some people plunge into sexual relationships hoping intimacy will follow, while others avoid being both intimate and sexual with the same person. Getting on the same page with your partner usually takes some effort.

Intimate Sexual Relationships

Intimacy takes place on a deep level. You are letting another person into a special place, letting yourself be seen and known. Becoming emotionally intimate with someone you are sexual with can be a frightening experience. Going the other direction, becoming sexual with someone you are already emotionally intimate with, can be equally frightening.

If you do feel afraid of or threatened by intimacy, you might respond by withdrawing or creating barriers between yourself and your sexual partner. You may distance yourself sexually, avoiding a deep sharing of your innermost self. Or you may allow yourself to share intimately while you're being sexual, but avoid vulnerability in your daily life.

You may find a certain level of intimacy comfortable in your sexual relationships, but panic when that relationship begins to grow and deepen. Notice if you feel compelled to test the strength of the relationship, to challenge your partner unnecessarily. Or you may overextend into the relationship, becoming obsessed with the approval of your partner rather than getting closer with them.

It is also commonly said that people with substance use disorders and trauma histories have severe problems expressing intimacy. When you consider the impact of gender, then the fear of intimacy that women, nonbinary people, and gender-expansive people may have is actually a well-grounded fear of emotional, physical, and sexual abuse. We know that women and girls from backgrounds that include out-of-control substance use are most likely to experience violence, abuse, and violation from those who have the closest proximity, like their friends, dating partners, and families. It is actually quite rational for women with substance use issues and/or prior traumatic experiences to fear intimacy; many have lived in situations in which their boundaries were violated by those who said "I love you."

The personal challenges you face to create an intimate, loving relationship are not insurmountable. Please remain gentle with yourself as you navigate the complexity of becoming close with another person. As you learn more about your own tendencies, you can turn your loving attention to those parts of you that still ask for healing and support.

It is important to remember that those who have a history of trauma and addiction often enter relationships that also have addictive qualities. Intimacy is mutual, respectful, and compassionate—but obsession, loss of self in the other, and other forms of passionate romantic intensity can be easily mistaken for intimacy.

The following chart may help you sort out the differences between an intimate and an addictive relationship. If you are in a relationship now, consider which column feels more descriptive of your connection. If you are not in a relationship now, think of your most recent relationship or a significant relationship from your past.

Contrasting Intimate Relationships and Addictive Relationships

Here is a description of the qualities of a loving, intimate relationship versus those of an addictive relationship.

Intimate Relationship	Addictive Relationship
Mutuality (shared, balanced)	Power over (controlling behavior)
Choice	Loss of choice
Freedom	Compulsion
Honesty, openness	Avoiding truth, lying
Desire to share needs and feelings	No-talk rule, especially if things are not working out.
Relationship is able to include growth and change.	Relationship is always the same.
I want to be there.	I have to be there.
I begin with me (self).	I begin with you.
Can say "I want" and "I feel"	You make me feel . . .
Active, not passive	Reactive
I take care of me. I am solely responsible for figuring out what I need and for communicating it to you.	You will know what's right for me and you will fix it.
Relationship deals with reality.	Relationship is based on delusion/fantasy.
Relationship deals with things as they are, whatever comes along.	Relationship uses denial and avoidance to deal with things.
I have a true interest in your personal/spiritual growth, even if it takes you away from me.	Your spiritual growth doesn't count.
Love is always an act of self-love.	Love is wanting someone with me at all costs.

Source: Adaptation of the text from pages 180–181 of *Leaving the Enchanted Forest* by Stephanie Covington and Liana Beckett.

6. When looking at this chart, what thoughts and feelings arise about the relationship you had in mind?

   What actions might you take to create more space for intimacy in your life?

   What actions might you take to create safety for yourself if intimacy is challenging?

If sexual desire and passion seemed easier to access in the past, know that you are not alone. Intimate sexual relationships create sexual connection from a foundation of safety, not confusion or danger, and this can take time to build or adjust to. Many people associate sexual feelings with stress, and our bodies respond powerfully to those associations.

It can help to remember that there are more types of sexual intimacy than any of us can imagine! You may have slow, sensual, eye-gazing lovemaking at one time, then raunchy, loud, messy sex another time, and any of the other infinite options as well. The key is that you trust your partner to show up with the intention of creating pleasure together, and you hold that intention as well. The exploration of what that means on any given day is yours to enjoy.

Somatic Practice: The Physiological Sigh

The following breathing technique has been shown to reduce acute stress quickly at almost any time. You can use it to calm yourself before a challenging conversation or to return to the present moment if your mind starts wandering while you are trying to be intimate with someone. You can also use it just before trying to sleep or during other stressful moments of your day.

The physiological sigh begins with a nearly full inhale through your nose. You then take a second short inhale through your nose, like a top-off of air. Exhale slowly through your mouth. If possible, the exhale should last longer than the inhales did.

Try this breathing pattern for three rounds. Inhale through the nose until your lungs are nearly full, then add a quick second inhale, then exhale slowly through your mouth.

Check in with your body and see if you can feel a difference.

CHAPTER 12

The Continuing Journey of Sexual Recovery

As a culture, we often confuse or have a limited idea of what pleasure is. I want to expand the idea of what pleasure is and highlight the tool and guide that it can be. Pleasure is not always something that, from beginning to end, makes us feel happy. If we look at pleasure in a more expansive way, pleasure can also mean contentment, satisfaction, quiet calmness, the fierce rush of internal movement toward coherence, or outward struggle against an adversary or challenge. . . . When we're committed to healing, committed to growth, committed to connection, and committed to pleasure there can be a kind of pleasure in doing anything.

Jamila Dawson, *With Pleasure: Managing Trauma Triggers for More Vibrant Sex and Relationships*, co-authored with August McLaughlin

Recovery is about expansion. It is about awakening to all that is possible in life. It is about integrating your inner life and your outer life, so that what's happening on the inside—your values, your beliefs, and your feelings—are being represented in your outer life, your actions with other people in the world. If your inner and outer lives are consistent, coherent, and congruent, you will experience integrity. For many, this integrity is the foundation of their spirituality.

Remember, we use the word *spirituality* as loosely as possible, to gesture at whatever way you stay connected to something greater than yourself. When talking about pleasure, sex, and relationships, we can easily forget that our most intimate, personal, and intense feelings are actually part of the larger world around us. Not only are we connected to all who have lived, loved, experienced pain, struggled with addiction, or survived trauma before us, but we are connected to thousands who are experiencing something similar in their own lives, right now.

Your sexuality is unique to you, and at the same time, it is part of what connects you to the world, people, environment, and social forces around you. Imagined this way, sexuality is inextricable from the energy of being alive.

We sometimes feel, and rightly so, that we have been trained to give up our sexuality in order to be more spiritual. Patriarchal religions dictate that our sexuality must be controlled by strict moral codes, and often reserved only for procreation. But what if we proceed from the belief that sexuality and spirituality are interconnected? They are both about the life force that is within us. They have enormous capacity to enrich our lives.

How you express your sexuality is your choice. If you choose to share your sexual self with another person, you are responsible for what you create together. Sexuality is a creative force, and you get to decide what kind of energy, relationship, or experience you want to bring into the world with your focused, present-moment attention. This chapter continues our reflections on intimacy, love, and deeper connections, with the goal of opening new directions for you in your ongoing recovery.

The Challenge of Safety

Emotional safety is the foundation of intimacy, and many of us struggle to find, build, or feel it. Tenderness is something we express most easily when we are feeling safe, and safety must be built through deliberate actions of care. If this sounds circular, remember the upward spiral. We return to the work of tending our relationships time and again.

Our healing begins with ourselves, but it can truly blossom only through connection with another person or people. If trauma happened in a relationship, then ultimately we need to feel a safe connection with other people to heal. We may grieve the end of our relationship with someone who harmed us, but then how do we learn to trust again?

We must address the specific challenges that arise for each one of us. Understanding our challenges, we see what we can do to communicate honestly, listen wholeheartedly, and navigate toward a deeper understanding and connection with the people in our lives now.

1. What makes it difficult for you to trust and feel safe with another person?

   What helps you trust and feel safe with another person?

2. What action(s) can you take on your own to create more safety for yourself and your sexuality? These actions may range from small to large, private to public. Perhaps you say a few affirming words to yourself, or join an online support group, or check out a few books on sexuality from the local library. Brainstorm a list of actions below, and then choose one action to take today.

   I can create more safety for myself and my sexuality by:

   Today's action: ______________________________ Date: __________

Conscious Love and Commitment

Choice is crucial to conscious love: The power and capacity to choose is what makes your intimacy authentic, and exercising that ability is basic to your recovery. Sex in any particular form is not the ultimate goal of sexuality, but it is one important facet in a complex expression of our whole being.

In choosing conscious love, you choose mature interdependence. You allow yourself truly to connect with and depend on your partner, but you retain your autonomy of self. You choose a partner who values your recovery and who also chooses to engage in the process with you. They are in a process of their own, and you mutually support one another's growth.

Choosing to be together is making a commitment. A loving commitment is not about the length of time you've been together; many of us know couples who have stayed together, without respect or mutuality, for decades. It is also not necessarily about monogamy or planning far into the future—these may or may not be aspects of a commitment, and they do not define it.

Loving commitment is about choosing to be there; to be intimate, open, and vulnerable; to do your best to be available to the other person while attending also to yourself. Loving commitment will allow you to feel safe and secure, knowing that the other has also chosen to be open, available, and vulnerable. Loving commitment requires choosing this not once, but again and again. The value of authentic, intimate sexual relationships is in their power to heal and change us. They empower us and cause us to grow.

3. Do you have concerns about engaging in conscious love and commitment? List them here.

Examples:

It's too late in my life for me to find the right person.

I don't think my partner is ready to do the emotional work for this.

I long for this kind of love so much that I'm afraid I'll scare someone off.

We are all going to have some concerns about love and commitment, and the concerns may feel overwhelming.

Still, the work is to be done in the present moment. Being committed means that you have promised to engage in a process with yourself and, if possible, your partner. The key is your willingness to be present with each other through the changes in your lives. You can learn to move into relationships gradually, both emotionally and physically. Slowly, bit by bit, the levels of emotional and physical intimacy and connection can deepen.

4. What commitments to yourself are you ready to make in service to creating more conscious love in your life? Try making three to five specific commitments.

   Examples:

   I commit to taking the time to know how I feel about sex before saying yes.

   I commit to asking my partner for reassurance when I am feeling afraid.

   I commit to my recovery, no matter what is happening in my relationship.

Ecstasy Is Real

Ecstatic sexual experience is one way for us to stay fully in the present moment and to appreciate how expansive it is. It does not usually happen by accident or without the work of real connection. In being sexual, we can meld with the other, losing the boundary of skin to skin, and exist in a sort of timelessness. Sometimes sexual ecstasy can even be our introduction to an authentic spiritual dimension in ourselves.

> ***Tamara***
> *Tamara had left her Christian upbringing behind when she came out as a lesbian in her late teens. The rupture with her family, especially her mother, was difficult. As far as Tamara was concerned, many decades later, spirituality had been a coercive force in her life, and she was not interested in reconnecting with it. However, she kept encountering people who believed that some form of spirituality was a crucial aspect of recovery. Then, she learned about the connection between mindfulness, meditation, and chronic pain.*

Tamara read articles about Black spiritual leaders like the Buddhist and civil rights activist Alvin Sykes. She turned her powerful curiosity toward the myriad ways Black Americans embodied spirituality, and she found many who had chosen the path of meditation. This emboldened her in her mindfulness practice.

She told her therapist that she had begun to sit in silence for a few minutes each day. "I don't sit on a cushion because of my back pain," she said. "I sit in a chair. I sometimes fall asleep. But I keep trying to just find a quiet place inside."

She signed up for a women's weekend meditation retreat, mostly on a whim.

Unexpectedly, she had an incredible time. She later shared with her recovery group that she had meditated for hours each day, sometimes in silence, sometimes walking, sometimes listening to teachings. Tamara found that while meditating, every now and then she could actually feel energy moving up and down her body, sometimes collecting in one place, other times staying in flow.

Another wonderful thing happened at that retreat: Tamara met someone she felt attracted to. Over the last dinner of the weekend, Tamara found out that Lucy enjoyed her company, too, and they began to spend time together back home. Their relationship developed slowly, with a deep foundation of mutual respect and friendship.

Tamara was joyful, for the first time in a long time. When she and Lucy were sexual, it was unlike any other experience she had had. "Sometimes when I'm with Lucy," she says, "I'm feeling something bigger than our physical bodies. I can't control when it is going to happen, although it's pretty clear when it won't—my pain is flaring up, or the stress of the day is too much. But when we are able to really relax into our intimacy, it sometimes feels like we are floating together, not two separate people, and I have this incredible sensation of warmth that envelops us."

This wonderful new experience came with some grief for Tamara, as she faced the reality that she had never been this vulnerable or present with Alisha, her ex-wife. At the same time, Tamara and Lucy, both in their sixties, rarely had the kind of spontaneous, urgent sex Alisha and Tamara had enjoyed in their forties.

"I'm learning to let go of my expectations," Tamara says. "Of course, I hope that I'll continue to have these sorts of experiences—both in sex and in meditation—but I've let go of them as goals. I love touching Lucy and being touched by her. Bonding with her feels special and precious. And if sometimes we enter another level of consciousness together, well," she smiles, "I'll take that gift."

5. What does *ecstasy* mean to you? Feel free to write or draw your answer.

Embracing the Pleasure of Change

Let's revisit a few important questions about sexuality as we reach our conclusion. As you answer these for yourself, recall how you may have answered them differently while you read chapter 1, versus now.

6. What does it mean to become a sexual person in our society?

   What does it mean to have this complex thing called sexuality integrated into our lives in a meaningful way?

What is your own unique experience of pleasure, and how do you cultivate it in a way that makes you feel glad to be alive?

Our interconnectedness is undeniable. Our ability to feel pleasure in the midst of chaotic circumstances, difficulty, and change is key to our resilience and connection to others. Sexuality is not fixed; it is a part of you that will change with you as you change. Embracing the pleasure of change begins with knowing where we have been.

At this time, you may want to turn back to the exercise Checking In with My Sexuality Today on pages 3 and 4, and see if any of your answers have shifted since you began.

7. Reading through your answers from the beginning of this workbook, what thoughts and feelings arise? What changes are you seeing?

The following twelve messages are drawn from the chapters you have just read and are offered here as note cards to take with you as you move along your upward spiral of recovery and healing.

8. After reading through all of the messages, choose one (or more) that stands out for you and write it down, exactly as it is or in your own words. Place this message somewhere you will see it, such as on a mirror or bedside table, or keep it private in your workbook.

    - It is possible for you to face what is unknown or painful about your own sexuality and grow into a new, loving relationship with this part of yourself.
    - What we seek is self-awareness, so we can be fully at choice whenever we are sexual.
    - No matter how much or how little spontaneous desire you feel, your unique sexuality can respond to pleasure.
    - You can live in a deeper state of acceptance, even gratitude, for your body, exactly as it is right now.
    - Looking honestly at your sexual past is essential to sexual recovery. Sometimes you will need a boost of courage to look at the reality of your life. Sometimes you will need permission to go slowly, rest, and recuperate.
    - It is normal to have some trouble identifying and asserting sexual limits and boundaries, because it is normal to have had insufficient or even harmful education about sexuality.
    - It is as important to take a long, careful look at your partners' behavior as it is to look at your own behavior. This is not because you can change them, but because you can see where you need to adjust your own boundaries and communication.
    - When you feel powerless, you can seek support. When you feel powerful, you can offer strength and support to yourself and others. An ebb and flow is to be expected.
    - Sexuality can become creative, a source of energy and interest, rather than a place of fear or numbness.
    - As we move toward establishing real intimacy in our lives, it becomes clear that intimacy with ourselves is our foundation for intimacy with others.
    - A great sexual relationship is nourishing, sustaining, pleasurable, and growth-fostering. It takes skill to maintain. The first skill is friendship.
    - Ongoing recovery is a process that circles around similar issues like an upward spiral. The work to be done is in the present moment, and as we move through our changes, more options for pleasure, connection, and intimacy open up.

Which message did you choose? What about this message is meaningful to you today?

As you decide what is next for you, we encourage you to take a few moments to fully celebrate the effort you put into awakening your sexuality.

9. How will you celebrate the effort you have put into awakening your sexuality?

   Examples:

   Light a candle and write a message of thanks to myself.

   Take a bath and touch my own body with appreciation.

   Wear a piece of clothing that makes me feel sexy and go out to dinner.

What is next for you in this process?

Examples:

There are some conversations I need to have with my partner.

I want to do some more sexual education.

I'm going to go back to a few of the exercises that were challenging and try again.

In a time of profound isolation, shame, and the normalization of hatred, the creation of loving connections with ourselves and others becomes ever more important. Sexuality can be such a powerful force in our lives, and it is our responsibility to face the personal past and make decisions now that reflect our desires and our integrity.

Our wish for you is this: When you are engaged in sexual connection, with yourself or others, may it be a source of joy for you. Enjoy the richness and variety of your unique sexuality as you grow and change over time. Your sensuality, eroticism, and sexuality can be a force for good.

NOTE CARDS

It is possible for you to face what is unknown or painful about your own sexuality and grow into a new, loving relationship with this part of yourself.

What we seek is self-awareness, so we can be fully at choice whenever we are sexual.

No matter how much or how little spontaneous desire you feel, your unique sexuality can respond to pleasure.

You can live in a deeper state of acceptance, even gratitude, for your body, exactly as it is right now.

NOTE CARDS

Looking honestly at your sexual past is essential to sexual recovery. Sometimes you will need a boost of courage to look at the reality of your life. Sometimes you will need permission to go slowly, rest, and recuperate.

It is normal to have some trouble identifying and asserting sexual limits and boundaries, because it is normal to have had insufficient or even harmful education about sexuality.

It is as important to take a long, careful look at your partners' behavior as it is to look at your own behavior. This is not because you can change them, but because you can see where you need to adjust your own boundaries and communication.

When you feel powerless, you can seek support. When you feel powerful, you can offer strength and support to yourself and others. An ebb and flow is to be expected.

NOTE CARDS

Sexuality can become creative,
a source of energy and interest,
rather than a place of fear or numbness.

As we move toward establishing real intimacy
in our lives, it becomes clear that intimacy
with ourselves is our foundation for
intimacy with others.

A great sexual relationship is nourishing,
sustaining, pleasurable, and growth-fostering.
It takes skill to maintain. The first skill
is friendship.

Ongoing recovery is a process that circles around
similar issues like an upward spiral. The work
to be done is in the present moment, and as
we move through our changes, more options for
pleasure, connection, and intimacy open up.

NOTES

CHAPTER 3

1. Emily Nagoski, *Come As You Are: The Surprising New Science That Will Transform Your Sex Life* (Simon & Schuster, 2021), 42–69.

CHAPTER 6

1. Douglas Braun-Harvey and Michael A. Vigorito, *Treating Out of Control Sexual Behavior: Rethinking Sex Addiction* (Springer, 2016), 28.

CHAPTER 9

1. Amy Vorenberg, Jessica Durkis-Stokes, and Jessica C. Brown, *Utmost Resistance: Examining Sexual Violence Law in the United States* (Carolina Academic Press, 2024), 122.

RESOURCES

Recovery Groups and Therapists

Please note: Some of these resources are free, and others have a membership fee or other cost. We list them here to offer you options to explore, not to recommend any particular program. If a program is based in the Twelve Step model developed by Alcoholics Anonymous, it will be noted.

LifeRing Secular Recovery
https://lifering.org/

Abstinence-based anonymous, secular meetings. Online and in person. All genders. No cost.

The Luckiest Club
https://www.theluckiestclub.com/
Dogma-free, compassionate place to recover from alcohol addiction and thrive in life. Online. All genders, with women's, LGBTQIA2S+, and BIPOC-only meetings. Monthly membership fee.

Manhattan Alternative
https://www.manhattanalternative.com/

Kink, poly, trans, and LGBTQ+-affirmative mental health providers. National online directory. Providers' fees will vary.

Moderation Management
https://moderation.org/

Behavior change program and peer-led support groups. Online. All genders. No cost.

Psychology Today Therapist Finder
https://www.psychologytoday.com/us
Online directory of individual therapists and support groups. Cost varies.

Sex and Love Addicts Anonymous (SLAA)
https://slaafws.org/

Online portal for the Twelve Step, Twelve Traditions–oriented fellowship (based on AA model) for those who desire to stop living out a pattern of sex and love addiction. Online and in-person meetings. Open to all, with gender-specific meetings available. No cost.

SHE RECOVERS Foundation
https://sherecovers.org/

Nonprofit movement for women. Online and facilitated groups, gatherings, and professional training. For women and nonbinary individuals, with meetings specific to LGBTQ+, BIPOC, veterans, mothers, and more. Meetings are free; other costs vary based on service.

The Small Bow
https://www.thesmallbow.com/

Newsletter, podcast, and online recovery meetings. All genders. Cost varies from free to subscription.

SMART Recovery
https://smartrecovery.org/

Evidence-informed approach to overcoming addictive behaviors. Online and in person. All genders. No cost.

Wombat Mental Health Services (for CA residents only)
https://wombatmhs.com/

Therapist-matching service providing equitable access to culturally appropriate, nonjudgmental, and affirmative mental health services for individuals from communities who have historically faced barriers in accessing care. All genders. Telehealth. Costs vary based on service and provider.

Women for Sobriety
https://womenforsobriety.org/

Peer-support program for women overcoming substance use disorders (SUDs). Online and in person. Women, nonbinary, and gender-expansive. No cost.

Sexuality, Bodies, and Pleasure

Allbodies
https://allbodies.com/

Online health classes that address sex, mental health, body literacy, and social justice. Costs vary per class.

OMGYES
https://www.omgyes.com/

Online library of instructional videos created from the largest research study into women's pleasure. Onetime payment for access to the library.

Planned Parenthood
https://www.plannedparenthood.org/learn/for-educators/digital-tools

Free sexuality education resources.

Books

Becoming Cliterate: Why Orgasm Equality Matters—and How to Get It by Laurie Mintz (HarperOne, 2017)

Better Sex Through Mindfulness: How Women Can Cultivate Desire by Lori A. Brotto (Greystone Books, 2018)

The Body Is Not an Apology: The Power of Radical Self-Love, 2nd ed., by Sonya Renee Taylor (Berrett-Koehler, 2021)

Body Neutral: A Revolutionary Guide to Overcoming Body Image Issues by Jessi Kneeland (Penguin Random House, 2023)

Come As You Are: The Surprising New Science That Will Transform Your Sex Life by Emily Nagoski, PhD (Simon & Schuster, 2021)

Disability Intimacy: Essays on Love, Care, and Desire edited by Alice Wong (Vintage, 2024)

Pleasure Activism: The Politics of Feeling Good edited by adrienne maree brown (AK Press, 2019)

Refusing Compulsory Sexuality: A Black Asexual Lens on Our Sex-Obsessed Culture by Sherronda J. Brown (North Atlantic Books, 2022)

Sensual Self: Prompts and Practices for Getting in Touch with Your Body by Ev'Yan Whitney (Clarkson Potter, 2021)

Sex for One: The Joy of Selfloving by Betty Dodson (Harmony, 2012)

Slow Pleasure: Explore Your Pleasure Spectrum by Euphemia Russell (Hardie Grant, 2022)

Want: Women's Fantasies in the Twenty-First Century edited by Gillian Anderson (Abrams, 2024)

"You Just Need to Lose Weight" and 19 Other Myths About Fat People by Aubrey Gordon (Beacon, 2023)

Relationships, Grief, and Healing

Books

All About Love: New Visions by bell hooks (William Morrow, 1999)

Decolonizing Nonviolent Communication, 2nd ed., by Meenadchi (Co—Conspirator Press, 2023)

Emotional Labor: The Invisible Work Shaping Our Lives and How to Claim Our Power by Rose Hackman (Flatiron Books, 2023)

It's OK That You're Not OK: Meeting Grief and Loss in a Culture That Doesn't Understand by Megan Devine (Sounds True, 2017)

Not That Bad: Dispatches from Rape Culture by Roxane Gay (Harper Perennial, 2018)

Sister Outsider: Essays and Speeches by Audre Lorde (Crossing Press, 2007)

Succulent Wild Woman: Dancing with Your Wonder-full Self! 25th Anniversary Edition by SARK (Atria Books, 2022)

With Pleasure: Managing Trauma Triggers for More Vibrant Sex and Relationships by August McLaughlin and Jamila Dawson, LMFT (Chicago Review Press, 2021)

The Wound Makes the Medicine: Elemental Remediations for Transforming Heartache by Pixie Lighthorse (Row House Publishing, 2023)

Domestic Violence Safety Planning

Domestic Violence Safety Plan
https://www.dvccct.org/wp-content/uploads/2020/03/Domestic-Violence-Safety-Plan-DVCC-.pdf

Checklist with hotlines to aid in escape, adapted from the Connecticut Coalition Against Domestic Violence's sample safety plan. Note that the National Domestic Violence Hotline is 800-799-7233; text 88788.

ABOUT THE AUTHORS

Stephanie S. Covington, PhD, LCSW (she/her), is an internationally recognized clinician, organizational consultant, lecturer, and author in the fields of addiction and trauma. Dr. Covington serves as the co-director of the Institute for Relational Development and the Center for Gender and Justice. For nearly four decades, she has created gender-responsive and trauma-informed programs and services for use in public, private, and institutional settings. Author of the first manualized treatment program for substance use disorder treatment, Dr. Covington went on to create twelve trauma-informed, gender-responsive treatment curricula. Her most recent works include the 30th anniversary edition of the bestseller *A Woman's Way Through the Twelve Steps* and *Hidden Healers: The Unexpected Ways Women in Prison Help Each Other Survive*.

www.stephaniecovington.com
www.centerforgenderandjustice.org

Vanessa Carlisle, PhD, MFA (they/them), is an author, coach, and educator in the fields of gender, sexuality, and trauma. Dr. Carlisle's lived experience includes over twenty-five years in sex work and fifteen years of advocacy for the sex-working community. As a survivor of both intimate partner and institutional violence, Dr. Carlisle now crafts programs that combat stigma and improve conditions for their communities, including trauma-informed self-defense training, somatic coaching, and end-of-life care services. Along with many essays and articles, Dr. Carlisle authored the award-winning novel *Take Me with You* about a queer sex worker who must face her grief to be able to build the life she wants.

www.vanessacarlisle.com

ALSO BY THE AUTHORS

By Stephanie S. Covington, PhD, LCSW

Becoming Trauma Informed: A Training for Staff Development

Beyond Anger and Violence+: A Program for Women and Gender-Diverse People

Beyond Trauma: A Healing Journey for Women

Beyond Violence+: A Prevention Program for Criminal Justice–Involved Women and Gender-Diverse People

Exploring Trauma+: Brief Intervention for Men and Gender-Diverse People with Shane S. Pugh and Roberto A. Rodriguez

Healing Trauma+: A Brief Intervention for Women and Gender-Diverse People with Eileen M. Russo

Helping Men Recover: A Program for Treating Addiction with Dan Griffin and Rick Dauer

Helping Men Recover: A Program for Treating Addiction (criminal justice edition) with Dan Griffin and Rick Dauer

Helping Women Recover: A Program for Treating Addiction

Helping Women Recover: A Program for Treating Addiction (criminal justice edition)

Hidden Healers: The Unexpected Ways Women in Prison Help Each Other Survive

Leaving the Enchanted Forest: The Path from Relationship Addiction to Intimacy with Liana Beckett

Moving from Trauma-Informed to Trauma-Responsive: A Training Program for Organizational Change with Sandra L. Bloom

Voices: A Program of Self-Discovery and Empowerment for Girls with Kimberley Covington and Madeline Covington

A Woman's Way Through the Twelve Steps

A Woman's Way Through the Twelve Steps Facilitator Guide

A Woman's Way Through the Twelve Steps Workbook

Women and Addiction: A Gender-Responsive Approach

Women in Recovery: Understanding Addiction

A Young Man's Guide to Self-Mastery with Roberto A. Rodriguez

By Vanessa Carlisle, PhD

Take Me with You

A Crack in Everything

I Was My Mother's Bridesmaid: Young Adults Talk About Thriving in a Blended Family with Erica Carlisle

PERMISSIONS

The following publishers or authors have given permission to use quotations in this book from copyrighted works (in order of appearance):

Emily Nagoski, "My Lying Vagina, and the Lying Liars Who Lie About Her," February 20, 2016, https://enagoski.medium.com/everyone-is-lying-about-the-vaginas-77038767238d.

Adrienne Rich, *On Lies, Secrets, and Silence: Selected Prose 1966–1978* (W.W. Norton, 1995), p. 189.

Judith V. Jordan, "Clarity in Connection: Empathic Knowing, Desire, and Sexuality," Wellesley Centers for Women, Wellesley College, 1986, p. 6, https://www.wcwonline.org/pdf/previews/preview_29sc.pdf.

Meenadchi, *Decolonizing Nonviolent Communication,* 2nd ed., self-published by Co—Conspirator Press with the support of Women's Center for Creative Work, 2021, p. 41.

SARK, author of *Succulent Wild Woman: Dancing with Your Wonder-full Self!* 25th Anniversary Edition, personal interview.

adrienne maree brown, *Pleasure Activism: The Politics of Feeling Good,* AK Press, 2019, pp. 122–123.

Jillian Weise, "Should You Send That Text," from *Cyborg Detective,* © 2019 by Jillian Weise, reprinted with the permission of The Permissions Company, LLC on behalf of BOA Editions, Ltd., boaeditions.org.

Sue Evans, MP, LP, "Relationship History Chart," adapted with the permission of the estate of Sue Evans.

ABOUT HAZELDEN PUBLISHING

As part of the Hazelden Betty Ford Foundation, Hazelden Publishing offers both cutting-edge educational resources and inspirational books. Our print and digital works help guide individuals in treatment and recovery, as well as their loved ones.

Professionals who work to prevent and treat addiction also turn to Hazelden Publishing for evidence-based curricula, digital content solutions, and videos for use in schools, treatment and correctional programs, and community settings. We also offer training for implementation of our curricula.

Through published and digital works, Hazelden Publishing extends the reach of healing and hope to individuals, families, and communities affected by addiction and related issues.